FREUDIANISM
A Critical Sketch

FREUDIANISM
A Critical Sketch

V. N. Vološinov

Translated by
I. R. TITUNIK

and edited in collaboration with
NEAL H. BRUSS

91-1570

INDIANA UNIVERSITY PRESS
Bloomington and Indianapolis

First Midland Book Edition 1987
Copyright © 1987 by Indiana University Press

Library of Congress Cataloging-in-Publication Data

Voloshinov, V. N.
    Freudianism: a critical sketch

    Translation of: Freĭdizm.
    Previous ed. published in 1976 as: Freudianism: a Marxist critique.
    Bibliography: p.
    Includes index.
    1. Psychoanalysis.   2. Freud, Sigmund, 1856–1939.
3. Subconsciousness.   4. Sex (Psychology)   5. Communism.
6. Psycholinguistics.   I. Title.
BF173.V6313   1987   150.19′52   87-45014
ISBN 0-253-20456-9 (pbk.)

1   2   3   4   5   91   90   89   88   87

Contents

Foreword by James V. Wertsch   *vii*
Translator's Introduction   *xv*

PART I   FREUDIANISM AND MODERN TRENDS IN
PHILOSOPHY AND PSYCHOLOGY
(CRITICAL ORIENTATION)

     Chapter 1   The Basic Ideological Motif of Freudianism   7
     Chapter 2   Two Trends in Modern Psychology   17

PART II   AN EXPOSITION OF FREUDIANISM

     Chapter 3   The Unconscious and the Dynamics of the
                 Psyche   29
     Chapter 4   The Content of the Unconscious   39
     Chapter 5   The Psychoanalytical Method   49
     Chapter 6   Freudian Philosophy of Culture   57

PART III   A CRITICAL ANALYSIS OF FREUDIANISM

     Chapter 7   Freudianism as a Variant of Subjective
                 Psychology   67
     Chapter 8   The Dynamics of the Psyche as a Struggle of
                 Ideological Motives and Not of Natural
                 Forces   75
     Chapter 9   The Content of Consciousness as Ideology   85

Appendix I   Discourse in Life and Discourse in Art (Concerning
               Sociological Poetics)   93
               V. N. Vološinov

Appendix II Chapter 10 A Critique of Marxist Apologias   117
                                      of Freudianism
                                      V. N. Vološinov

Appendix III V. N. Voloshinov and the Basic Assumptions   133
                         of *Freudianism* and Structuralism
                         Neal H. Bruss

Index   *145*

Foreword

JAMES V. WERTSCH

Freudianism: A Critical Essay was written in what is perhaps the most exciting intellectual milieu the twentieth century has known—the Soviet Union between the October Revolution and the onset of the Stalinist purges in the late 1930s.[1] During these years a whirlwind of creative energy changed virtually every aspect of that country's intellectual and cultural life. Among the sciences transformed was psychology, which was given the tasks of specifying the criteria for a Marxist account of mind and using these criteria to organize concrete research.

In the debates of those years, one of the major issues was whether or not a theory of mind was immediately discernible in the writings of Marx, Engels, and Lenin. Some psychologists claimed that it was and that the task confronting them was how to mine these writings in the most appropriate manner. Most Soviet scholars, however, argued that a genuine Marxist approach would have to draw on existing theories of psychology (both from the Soviet Union and abroad) as well as on Marxist texts to create the theory they sought. For those who accepted this line of reasoning, the issue became one of translating Marxist tenets into concrete, detailed claims about psychology. This is what Zinchenko and Smirnov (1983) view as a central "methodological" task of Soviet psychology.

In order to carry out this methodological task, Soviet psychology relied extensively on ideas developed at home (i.e., in prerevolutionary Russian, as well as Soviet, psychology), but as I have noted elsewhere (Wertsch, 1985a, 1985b), they also drew extensively on theories developed in the West. *Freudianism* may be viewed as one of the attempts to draw on, and react to, ideas from "bourgeois" psychology in order to formulate a Soviet Marxist approach to mind.

At the time *Freudianism* was being written, several other attempts were underway in the USSR to create *the* Marxist psychology. In the charged intellectual and political atmosphere of the 1920s and early 1930s there were heated disputes over the proper course to follow in carrying out this task, but certain characteristics tend to appear in all of these attempts. The first such characteristic is the seemingly aggressive arrogance displayed toward other Soviet authors, and especially toward "bourgeois" psychologists. To some extent this style can be found today in Soviet writings, but it was much more prevalent during the twenties and thirties. What is the source of this tone and why was it so evident during those years? There are several answers, the first of which is that the arrogance reflects the general style of debate among the Russian intelligentsia (both before and after the revolution), but I think its prevalence during those early years indexes another factor. This goes back to the intellectual whirlwind mentioned above. Soviet scholars in psychology as well as in other disciplines were convinced that they were building the society of the future; hence they had little patience for old ways of thinking. In their view these old ways of thinking were reflections of the outmoded social formation, namely capitalism, in which psychology had evolved up to that point. Although there are probably no major schools of psychology in the world today that display the kind of certainty and enthusiasm found in a work such as *Freudianism*, these feelings pervaded a great deal of what the young scholars were saying at the time in the USSR.

If this conveys something of the tone of the argument over what a Marxist psychology should be, what are some of the points of substance? The issues of substance I shall address are not ones that Soviet psychologists of that era had the option of confronting or ignoring. They are methodological dictates that had to be addressed in one way or another if a theory was to be taken seriously in the ongoing debate about what constituted an adequate Marxist psychology. Two basic methodological dictates are reflected in *Freudianism*: first, that a Marxist psychology must deal with the cultural and historical specificity of human consciousness; and, second, that a Marxist psychology must be grounded in objective methods.

With regard to the cultural and historical specificity of human consciousness, it is worth noting that *Freudianism* was far ahead of its time. Even now, more than a half century after its publication, this issue has not been adequately addressed in psychology in the West. In the USSR, several schools of psychology at least recognized it as a basic issue to be addressed in an adequate account of mental processes. The basic claim here is that a psychology should be able to specify what distinguishes the mental processes of people from different cultural and historical contexts. For example, such a psychology should be able to specify how the thinking of a Soviet in the late twentieth century differs from the thinking of an American of the same period or from the thinking of a Russian peasant of the eighteenth century. To the extent that these issues have been addressed, they have been addressed in sociology, anthropology, and history, but psychology has had very little to say about them.

Much of what Voloshinov has to say in *Freudianism* is motivated by this claim. From the outset he criticizes Freud for grounding his theory in universal, ahistorical constants, namely, sex and age.[2] Instead of viewing psychic dynamics as growing out of a struggle of natural forces, Voloshinov argues that they reflect a struggle of socioculturally constituted, and hence socioculturally specific, motives; for him, "the human psyche and consciousness reflect the dialectics of history to a much greater degree than the dialectics of nature" (p. 83).

In Voloshinov's opinion Freud's ahistorical approach to psychic dynamics stemmed from the specific milieu in which the latter lived and worked. The author of

Freudianism thought that the biological reductionism generally characteristic of the Western human sciences and philosophy of the time reflected a defensiveness toward social change, or, conversely, an unwillingness to recognize the "disintegration and decline of the bourgeois world" (p. 14). It is in this connection that Voloshinov devotes his first chapter to the "ideological motif of Freudianism."

Although some of the specifics of this critique by Voloshinov are not particularly convincing, the general assumption behind it is quite interesting and important. This assumption is that cultural and historical contexts influence the investigator as well as the subjects being investigated. This is an assumption that is appreciated by scholars in several disciplines (e.g., in the case of literature, see Clark and Holquist, 1984), but it has only recently begun to be taken seriously in psychology (cf. Meacham, 1984; Wertsch and Youniss, in press). Hence Voloshinov's ideas on this issue have contemporary relevance for psychology rather than being a historical footnote.[3]

Turning to the methodological dictate of using objective methods, we again see that Voloshinov had a great deal critical to say about Freud. As was the case with claims about the cultural and historical specificity of mind, calls for an objective method were an essential part of the underlying assumptions with which Soviet psychology was operating. Soviet scholars had a deep, even radical commitment to science as the means for explicating and solving all sorts of problems. This was of course largely a reflection of Marxism's claims about being a scientific approach to social issues. It was also a part of the continuing reaction against any hint of the idealism and spiritualism that had played a role in prerevolutionary Russian psychology.

Voloshinov's call for objective methods was motivated by the desire to create an objective, materialist psychology *without* falling prey to physiological reductionism.[4] In other words, Voloshinov insisted on using objective methods to investigate phenomena such as mind and consciousness that are inaccessible or disallowed in physiological or strict behaviorist accounts. This all occurred in the context of the "struggle for consciousness" that L. S. Vygotsky (1934) and others were waging during those same years.

Voloshinov's argument, however, represents a bold and unique position in this struggle for consciousness because, unlike other approaches, it begins with a fundamentally social epistemology. Whereas other psychological theories of the time were reaching toward the social, Voloshinov viewed social activity as the category from which all else flowed. Furthermore, he focused on large-scale social dynamics (e.g., societal power relations) that shape individual consciousness but are not explainable on the basis of individual psychology and are even beyond the normal purview of individual consciousness. For Voloshinov to use this social epistemology as the basis for reinterpreting Freud's notion of the unconscious was a radical move indeed. It attacked an idea that is inherently psychological in Freud's account by shifting from a psychologistic to a social framework. It is indicative of the fact that in Voloshinov's view the activity that most fundamentally defines us as human is to be found on the social, rather than the individual plane. Furthermore, it focused on aspects of the social that no other theory of psychology had tackled.

The key to carrying out this complex task for Voloshinov was the semiotic analysis of human communication. It was this analysis that allowed him to conduct objective research on human mental processes while never losing sight of his call for cultural and historical specificity. At the core of this analysis is the claim that any utterance in human communication is an irreducibly social phenomenon. This means that attempts to explicate the meaning or form of an utterance by turning to the individual are misguided; in Voloshinov's view, "Every utterance is *the product of the interaction between speakers* and the product of the broader context of the whole complex *social situation* in which the utterance emerges" (p. 79). This social situation can be analyzed at various levels. On the one hand it can be viewed in terms of the "*immediate* small social event—the event of communication, of exchange of words between persons" (p. 86). This is the focus of chapter 8 of *Freudianism*. On the other hand, it involves the "broader, more enduring and steadfast social connections . . . the whole repertoire of value judgments, points of view, approaches, and so on" (p. 86) that are the concern of chapter 9. Phenomena at either of these levels are amenable to objective investigation.

Like Vygotsky (1934), Voloshinov argued that the kinds of dynamics involved in social communication are the source of individual mental processes. It is in this connection that his ideas on inner speech take on such importance. Inner speech is a specific mechanism that makes it possible to explicate how and why human mental processes are fundamentally social. In a nutshell the argument is that if mental processes are mediated by language and if language is inherently social, then mental processes are necessarily social in nature.

Although there appears to have been little contact between members of the Bakhtin Circle and Vygotsky (but see the footnote on page 21), the ideas of the latter complement several points Voloshinov made in *Freudianism* and in *Marxism and the Philosophy of Language* (1929) quite nicely. Taken together, the two authors' ideas on inner speech provide a coherent way to deal with Voloshinov's dictum that "*human* psychology must be *socialized*" (p. 22).

Vygotsky's contribution to this overall picture begins with his claims about the social origins of inner speech in ontogenesis. In a series of empirical studies conducted during the 1920s and early 1930s Vygotsky (1934) examined the ways in which children (roughly between three and seven years of age) speak aloud to themselves as they are engaged in activities such as drawing. This is the speech form Piaget (1926) had labeled "egocentric." *Contra* Piaget, who had argued that egocentric speech is an index of children's as yet unsocialized thought and hence a speech form that dies out with age, Vygotsky argued that egocentric speech is a transitional semiotic form between external, social speech and inner speech. Hence its fate is to "go underground" rather than to die out. In a series of ingenious studies he demonstrated that egocentric speech reflects an ongoing differentiation between social speech and speech for oneself. Among other things, he showed that during this functional differentiation egocentric speech continues to reflect its social origins in several telltale ways. For example, its incidence is higher in what appear to the child to be social, communicative situations (even though no social interaction in fact occurs) than in settings where the child is isolated from others.

In general, Vygotsky's approach to egocentric speech and other semiotic mechanisms mediating human mental functioning (cf. Wertsch, 1985b) is entirely consistent with Voloshinov's analysis and fills in some important gaps in what he and other members of the Bakhtin Circle had to say. Voloshinov and others, in turn, dealt with several issues that are left implicit or underspecified in Vygotsky's writings. The most important of these is the cultural and historical contextualization of social life and hence of mental processes. As already noted, Voloshinov's account of the social focuses much more than others' accounts on issues of politics and power. Vygotsky made his claims about the social origins of egocentric and inner speech in such a way that there is little reason to deal with these issues or to distinguish one cultural-historical context from another. This is because his account of social action focused almost entirely on microsociological, face-to-face communication. Thus, he had relatively little to say about issues such as class struggle and forms of consciousness that are associated with specific social formations.

Voloshinov deals with these issues in *Freudianism* by trying to locate his semiotic analysis in an approach that was basically concerned with political and social power. This necessarily involved the assumption that certain dimensions of social interaction and semiotic processes vary, depending on cultural-historical context. Thus, in addition to examining how an utterance reflects the *"immediate* small social event"* of which it is a part, he insists on taking into account the "broader, more enduring and steadfast social connections out of whose dynamics are generated all elements of the form and content of our inner and outward speech" (p. 86). This is a step that is consistent with what Vygotsky had to say, but with the exception of a few of his passing comments on the cultural specificity of inner speech, it goes beyond what Vygotsky actually covered in his writings.

Power relations emerge for Voloshinov as an issue both at the level of discourse in the "immediate small social event" and on the level of "broader, more enduring and steadfast social connections." In the end it is essential to recognize both of these interconnected levels if one is to understand how hierarchies of power are constituted, instantiated, and perpetuated. His line of reasoning on this issue is reflected most clearly in his radical reinterpretation of Freud's conscious and unconscious processes. He begins by arguing that their "mutual hostility and incomprehension" (p. 77) actually reflect "two ideas, two ideological trends, two antagonistic persons, and not . . . two natural, material forces" (p. 77). In Voloshinov's view the "hostility and incomprehension" at issue are in the end facts about the doctor and patient in concrete communicative contexts. In addition, however, Voloshinov viewed antagonisms between particular doctors and patients as indices of broader social relations (e.g., class relations) in society at large.

Discourse is like a "scenario" of the immediate act of communication in the process of which it is engendered, and this act of communication is, in turn, a factor of the wider field of communication of the community to which the speaker belongs. In order to understand this "scenario," it is essential to reconstruct all those complex social inter-relations of which the given utterance is the ideological refraction. (p. 79)

These points apply equally, in Voloshinov's opinion, to external social speech and to inner speech.

Nothing changes at all if, instead of outward speech, we are dealing with inner speech. Inner speech, too, assumes a listener and is oriented in its construction toward that lis-tener. Inner speech is the same kind of product and expression of social intercourse as is outward speech. (p. 79)

Thus, Voloshinov's emphasis on social factors does not reflect a lack of concern with the psychological; it just means that in his view social activity is the fundamen-tal category and that psychological activity can be understood only by understand-ing the social. He develops this view as an antidote to Freud's, which "*projects* the entire dynamics of the interrelationship between two people into the individual psyche" (p. 80).

Because Voloshinov explicates social relations such as those between doctor and patient in terms of class struggle as outlined in Marxist texts of his time, many of his comments are not particularly interesting from today's perspective. In other writings by the Bakhtin Circle, especially by Bakhtin himself, the mechanisms whereby social and inner speech forms reflect cultural-historical differences are explicated in a more complete and interesting way. Already in *Freudianism,* however, one can find the seeds of Bakhtin's argument in some points concerning the nature of the utterance. In chapter 8 Voloshinov touches on these issues by stating that "Every utterance is *the product of the interaction between speakers* and the product of the broader context of the whole complex *social situation* in which the utterance emerges" (p. 79), and in "Discourse in Life and Discourse in Art" he goes further in his analysis of the utter-ance. There he argues that "*any locution actually said aloud or written down for intelligible communication* (i.e., anything but words merely reposing in a dictionary) *is the expression and product of the social interaction of three participants: the speaker* (author), *the listener* (reader), and *the topic* (the who or what) *of speech* (the hero)" (p. 105). The points made in this quote touch on the core of what Bakhtin was to go on to explicate in many of his writings (e.g., Bakhtin, 1963, 1965, 1981): his emphasis on concrete discourse as opposed to abstract linguistic form; his insistence on focusing on how author, hero, and reader interact; and his notions of alterity and otherness (cf. Todorov, 1984; Clark and Holquist, 1984). By harnessing these ideas, he was able to provide brilliant insights into issues such as how voices from various social strata come into contact and how the relationship between author, hero, and reader has changed over the history of novelistic discourse.

Freudianism is not all that convincing in many of its specific criticisms of psycho-analysis, mainly because it is overly polemical, insufficiently specific, and at certain points simply outdated. It is, however, an important volume, and an important volume from today's perspective. In many respects it goes beyond most treatments today of the relationship between the psychological and the social. Furthermore, it represents an important step in the Bakhtin Circle's attempt to explore the social and semiotic forces that underlie human consciousness. For example, in its analysis of discursive political processes it sets the stage for the arguments advanced in *Marxism and the Philosophy of Language*.

Taken by itself, *Freudianism* may not generally be regarded as one of the most important works produced by the Bakhtin Circle. However, it must play a central role in attempts to understand the brilliant insights produced by this group. There is little doubt that as we continue to delve deeper into these insights we will find ourselves returning again and again to this volume where many of them began to take on life.

Notes

1. Beginning with V. V. Ivanov's (1974) comments, there has been a great deal of discussion over whether V. N. Voloshinov wrote this text alone, co-authored it with M. M. Bakhtin, or had it published under his name after Bakhtin had written it (e.g., Clark and Holquist, 1984; Titunik, 1987; Todorov, 1984). I think there is convincing evidence that Bakhtin at least had a hand in writing *Freudianism*, although the evidence in this case (especially the style and content of the text) is less convincing in my opinion than in the case of *Marxism and the Philosophy of Language* (1973), which was also published under the name of Voloshinov. In the spirit of Bakhtinian multivoicedness I would like to express my appreciation to Michael Holquist for his comments on an earlier draft of this introduction.

2. Some of Freud's works dealing with sociocultural themes (e.g., *Civilization and Its Discontents*, 1961) were not available to Voloshinov at the time the latter was writing *Freudianism*. Had they been, Voloshinov may have taken a somewhat different tack, but his basic critique concerned with the cultural and historical specificity of human mental processes would nonetheless have remained largely the same.

3. It should be noted that the goal of self-critically situating psychological theories in their cultural and historical contexts is as unrealized in the USSR as it is in the West. Even though Marxist social theory has led Soviet scholars to recognize the importance of this issue, they have not produced a detailed, convincing analysis of the cultural-historical specificity of theories in their own or any other society. Indeed, the work of scholars such as Bauer (1952) shows that Soviet psychological theory sometimes reflects its social and political context more uncritically than is the case in Western approaches.

4. Such reductionism was to plague Soviet approaches in the 1940s and early 1950s. It was subsequently branded "vulgar materialism" by Soviet scholars.

References

Bakhtin, M. M. (1981). *The dialogic imagination: Four essays by M. M. Bakhtin*. Edited by M. Holquist; translated by C. Emerson and M. Holquist. Austin: University of Texas Press.

Bakhtin, M. M. (1963). *Problemy poetiki Dostoevskogo*. [Problems of Dostoevsky's poetics] Moscow: Sovetskii Pisatel: Revised and expanded version of *Problemy tvorchestva Dos-*

toevskogo [Problems of Dostoevsky's creative works] published in 1929. *Problems of Dostoevsky's poetics.* Edited and translated by C. Emerson. 1984. Minneapolis: University of Minnesota Press.

Bakhtin, M. M. (1965). *Tvorchestvo Fransua Rable i narodnaya kul'tura srednevekov'ya i Renessansa* [The work of Francois Rabelais and popular culture of the Middle Ages and the Renaissance. *Rabelais and his world.* Translated by Hélène Iswolsky. 1968. Cambridge, MA: MIT Press. Reprinted, 1984. Bloomington: Indiana University Press.

Bauer, R. A. (1952). *The new man in Soviet psychology.* Cambridge, MA: Harvard University Press.

Clark, K., and Holquist, M. (1984). *Mikhail Bakhtin.* Cambridge, MA.: Harvard University Press.

Freud, S. (1961) *Civilization and its discontents.* New York: Norton. First published in German in 1930.

Ivanov, V. V. (1974). The significance of M. M. Bakhtin's ideas on sign, utterance, and dialogue for modern semiotics. In H. Baran (ed.), *Semiotics and structuralism: Readings from the Soviet Union.* White Plains, NY: International Arts and Sciences Press.

Meacham, J. A. (1984). The individual as consumer and producer of historical change. In McCloskey and H. W. Reese (eds.), *Life-span developmental psychology: Historical and generational effects.* New York: Academic Press.

Piaget, J. (1926). *The language and thought of the child.* New York: Harcourt.

Titunik, I. R. (1987) Translator's Introduction to V. N. Voloshinov. *Freudianism: A critical sketch.* 1987. Bloomington: Indiana University Press.

Todorov, T. (1984). *Mikhail Bakhtin: The Dialogical Principle.* Translated by W. Godzich. Minneapolis: University of Minnesota Press.

Voloshinov, V. N. (1929). *Marksizm i filosofiya yazyka: Osnovnye problemy sotsiologicheskogo metoda v nauke o yazyke* [Marxism and the philosophy of language: Basic problems of the sociological method in the science of language]. Leningrad: Priboi. *Marxism and the philosophy of language.* 1973. Translated by L. Matejka and I. R. Titunik. New York: Seminar Press. Reprinted, 1986. Cambridge, MA: Harvard University Press.

Vygotsky, L. S. (1934). *Myshlenie i rech: Psikhologicheskie issledovaniya* [Thinking and speech: Psychological investigations]. Moscow and Leningrad: Gosudarstvennoe Sotsial'no-Ekonomicheskoe Izdatel'stvo. Abridged translation: *Thought and language.* 1962. Cambridge, MA: MIT Press; complete translation: *Thinking and speech.* 1987. New York: Plenum.

Wertsch, J. V. (1985a). Introduction to J. V. Wertsch (ed.), *Culture, communication, and cognition: Vygotskian perspectives.* New York: Cambridge University Press.

Wertsch, J. V. (1985b). *Vygotsky and the social formation of mind.* Cambridge, MA: Harvard University Press.

Wertsch, J. V., and Youniss, J. (in press). Contextualizing the investigator: The case of developmental psychology. *Human development.*

Zinchenko, V. P., and Smirnov, S. D. (1983). *Metodologicheskie voprosy psikhologii* [Methodological problems in psychology]. Moscow: Izdatel'stvo Moskovskogo Universiteta.

Translator's Introduction

Frejdizm: kritičeskij očerk [Freudianism: A Critical Sketch] was published in the year 1927 by the State Publishing House, Moscow-Leningrad. The name of the author was V[alentin] N[ikolaevič] Vološinov (1895–1936), under whose authorship articles on music, psychology, and the theory of language and literature had previously appeared in print, starting in 1922, and several other works, most notably the book *Marksizm i filosofija jazyka: osnovnye problemy sociologičeskogo metoda v nauke o jazyke* [Marxism and the Philosophy of Language: The Basic Problems of the Sociological Method in the Study of Language], were subsequently to appear over the years 1928–30.[1] None of these publications or their author received any appreciable attention at the time, and they remained in virtual oblivion for the next three decades. An important exception to this general neglect was provided by one of the most eminent linguists and thinkers of modern times, Roman Jakobson. The young Jakobson knew and was intrigued by *Marksizm i filosofija jazyka*, particularly struck by certain of its ideas regarding the operations of reported speech. In the 1930s Jakobson's enthusiasm was communicated to fellow members of the Prague Linguistic Circle.[2] Later, after his move to the United States, Jakobson referred to Vološinov's book and employed its ideas about reported speech in his seminal treatise, *Shifters, Verbal Categories, and the Russian Verb*.[3] And it was also Jakobson who, in the early 1970s, played the key role in bringing about the English translation of *Marksizm i filosofija jazyka*.[4] Still, even at the time that translation appeared and despite Jakobson's interest and influence, Vološinov and his works remained in obscurity, information about them and about the intellectual milieu to which they belonged being, to say the least, scant.

Meanwhile, however, other things were happening. The now world famous Russian scholar Mixail Mixajlovič Baxtin (1895–1975), whose book on Dostoevskij[5] had had considerable success on its publication in 1929 but who that very same year had been sent into exile (in Soviet Central Asia), began to be "rehabilitated" in the 1960s. At first it was mainly the then newly emerging structuralist wing of Soviet humanistic studies that promoted the revival of attention to Baxtin, but that attention was soon to become widespread throughout the entire Soviet intellectual community. A second, revised and supplemented, edition in 1963 of his book on Dostoevskij and then the long delayed publication of his dissertation on Rabelais in 1965[6] functioned as signs of and as stimulants to the new, very much revitalized and expanded interest in Baxtin.

In 1971 a public meeting was held at Moscow University in honor of Baxtin's seventy-fifth birthday. A report of the speeches given at that meeting appeared in the second issue for 1971 of the journal *Voprosy jazykoznanija* (pp. 160–62). Among other matters, information was supplied in that report regarding a relationship between Baxtin and V. N. Vološinov (and others, including Pavel Nikolaevič Medvedev (1891–1941), all of whom are now commonly referred to as the "Baxtin circle"). Two years later, in the published version of his celebratory address on Baxtin's seventy-fifth birthday, the distinguished Soviet linguist and semiotician V. V. Ivanov announced (in a footnote to the bibliography of Baxtin's works appended to his article) that works signed by V. N. Vološinov and also by P. N. Medvedev had in fact been written by Baxtin (the book *Frejdizm* was included in his list).[7] Although Ivanov advanced no proof for this contention, merely alluding to the existence of proof, and although no public statement on the matter was made by Baxtin himself, either then or ever, the attribution of works signed by Vološinov and Medvedev to Baxtin was immediately widely accepted. Thus, from that point on, for a very considerable part of the community of scholars, writings signed by Vološinov and Medvedev have been amalgamated together with the writings signed by Baxtin into one magisterial oeuvre under Baxtin's name and, as such, have received a growing appreciation, both within the Soviet Union and, especially, in the Western world; indeed, in most recent years, the Baxtin so represented enjoys an ever more massive and intensive international interest throughout the entire domain of humanistic studies.

On the face of it, that appears to settle matters: Vološinov and Medvedev, as it were, evaporate, leaving behind an all-congealing Baxtin. But there are a number of nagging unsolved problems that make it—or, at any rate, should make it—impossible to accept such a resolution with equanimity, as has been done by the majority of interested persons. For one thing, it ought to be made clear that the case for attribution does not rest at any point on established facts. The seemingly simple question as to what is supposed actually to have happened—when, where, why, under what circumstances, with what kind of agreement, whether with or without collaboration, etc., etc., Baxtin supposedly produced the writings signed by others—remains unanswered to the present day. Although the events in question belong mainly to the not so remote 1920s and although certain participants and witnesses remained alive until quite recent times, including Baxtin himself, and although the matter has been researched by highly qualified investigators with access to the realm of Baxtiniana and its denizens, no one has so far been able to provide anything like an authentic account of what really happened. Instead, operating on the basis of hearsay and circumstantial evidence and employing the instruments of speculation, surmise, and ingenuity, various proponents of Baxtin's authorship of the "disputed works" have come up with sundry scenarios, not one, or any combination, of which has been concretely substantiated. Such speculative scenarios are, of course, perfectly legitimate in the absence of facts, but they do not have, and ought not be taken as having, the status and authority of facts. Due to the apparent unobtainability or nonexistence of solid evidence and also due to the paranoiac secrecy inherent in the Soviet *modus vivendi et operandi* (whose application in this particular instance is itself a conundrum), the actual facts of the matter in question here in all likelihood will never be known.[8]

However, the facts, as such, do not constitute the whole issue; and what is at stake, in any case, is no mere legalistic matter of property rights. Attribution to Baxtin of writings signed by Vološinov and Medvedev creates certain methodological, conceptual, and ideological puzzles. The amalgamation of all of the writings in question into a single Baxtinian recension has been accomplished most typically by ignoring or minimizing all differential features setting the writings signed by Vološinov and Medvedev off from those signed by Baxtin. While this Translator's Introduction is hardly the place to engage in close and detailed argument about a matter so complex and perplexing, the reader ought at least be made aware that there is a problem (a point often overlooked elsewhere) and given some notion as to what it involves.[9]

Among the various factors in that problem, one so blatant as to suggest something in the mode of "The Emperor's New Clothes" has to do with the explicitly espoused and implemented Marxist orientation of the writings signed by Vološinov and Medvedev and the conspicuous absence of any such orientation in the writings signed by Baxtin. In the argument over the attribution of the former works to Baxtin this discrepancy must figure as a vital question to be confronted and resolved. The attempt to do so, however, encounters the most bewildering and irreconcilable assortment of opinions. The chief proponents of Baxtin's authorship of the disputed works writing and publishing in the Soviet Union (S. Bočarov, S. Averincev, S. Konkin, V. Kožinov, V. Ivanov, Ju. Lotman et al.) have remained startlingly silent on the question of Baxtin's Marxist credentials in connection with the evident Marxist intentions of the works attributed to him. Such silence under such circumstances allows of only one interpretation: those credentials and intentions are being implicitly denied. Precisely this denial is made explicit outside the Soviet Union by those Western scholars for whom the Marxism of the works attributed to Baxtin is nothing more than "expedience" and "disguise," a necessary but ultimately meaningless pretence undertaken for the sake of making those works acceptable for the Soviet press. This is the majority view, most emphatically exposited by the American Baxtin expert Michael Holquist,[10] and the view to which even Roman Jakobson, in the last years of his life, also subscribed. However, other interested persons, particularly the Marxist scholar Helmut Glück, have concluded that the Marxist orientation of the writings signed by Vološinov and Medvedev is too genuine and vital and the absence of such an orientation in the writings signed by Baxtin too patent to permit acceptance of the attribution of the former writings to Baxtin.[11] Yet, quite a different conclusion is reached by other Marxist spokesmen such as M. Yaguello, R. Matijašević, and F. Jameson who hail the Baxtin not only of the attributed works, but of his own signed writings as well, as an outstanding Marxist writer and thinker.[12] Finally, there are still others like

Tzvetan Todorov who, while preferring the idea of a single, unified Baxtinian system, do admit that the ideological discrepancy between the attributed works and the works signed by Baxtin constitutes a serious and troubling aberration in that system.[13]

These varying and contradictory opinions regarding the question of Marxism in the Baxtin legacy surely point up a problem whose resolution would seem logically of primary importance: Without agreeing on their ideological orientation, how are we properly to understand and appreciate and ourselves make use of the ideas which come to us under disparate auspices but as supposedly belonging to one and the same thinker? After all, the similar ideas we find featured in the writings signed by Vološinov and Medvedev, on the one hand, and in the writings signed by Baxtin himself, on the other, may, if ideologically oriented in different ways, be subject to quite different interpretations. For instance, the concept of *dialogue,* so central for all three signatories, must operate differently in a materialistic monist conception of things—and precisely such a conception is explicitly espoused in the Vološinov and Medvedev writings—than in the sometimes dualist, sometimes pluralist outlook which Baxtin, in his signed writings, seems to have favored. May it not be possible, then, that the amalgamation of all the writings in question together into a single Baxtinian recension, into a "Baxtin legacy," produces something on the order of an ideological Frankenstein Monster? Even in the least likely hypothesis that Baxtin was himself a Marxist in everything he wrote, the question remains pertinent, seeing that, in one case, the Marxism is openly declared and directly engaged, whereas in the other, the Marxism is invisible and requires a special kind of analysis and interpretation to be made manifest.

Furthermore, even superficial inspection of the two sets of writings is sufficient to detect obvious differences in style of presentation and in technical concerns. As regards the latter, the technical concerns of the professional linguist in Vološinov's case (especially with respect to the problem of reported speech) and the technical concerns of the professional literary critic in Medvedev's (especially as concerns the program for sociological poetics) are not matched in the signed works of Baxtin. Indeed, it has more than once been acknowledged of Baxtin that the "technical aspect" was always a "secondary matter" for him.[14] As regards the factor of style, one can point to, among other things, such features as humor, sarcasm, and all manner of polemical procedures as characteristic of the Vološinov and Medvedev writings but wholly absent from writings signed by Baxtin. These factors do not, of course, make it impossible that Baxtin did actually write the disputed works, but those factors do, in their turn, bring a rather tricky question to the fore: If Baxtin did write those works in the style and in the technical registers of their signatories, as well as with their ideological orientation, then are we dealing with something like "disguise," as is generally alleged, or with something more like extreme stylization or even, in principle, "forgery"?

All such misgivings and doubts as have been mentioned here, and others that have not been,[15] supply sufficient grounds, in my opinion, to be skeptical regarding the attribution of the works signed by Vološinov and Medvedev to Baxtin. This specifically, of course, applies to the work presented in translation here. There are certain interested persons, also with misgivings and doubts, who prefer the compromise of designating the author of *Frejdizm*, and of all the other disputed works, by using the coupling of names (however, never with an "and" but only with a hyphen or a slash between them, e.g., Baxtin-Vološinov or Baxtin/Vološinov, thereby leaving a certain loophole). In view of the fact that V. N. Vološinov was originally named the author of *Frejdizm: kritičeskij očerk* and that nothing has conclusively proved that he was not, I see no reason to follow that practice and I prefer to retain Vološinov's name alone as author in this translation. Elementary integrity would seem to dictate that changes of past history be made, not by fiat or majority rule, but only when it is conclusively proved that what we thought was true is wrong. That has not happened so far in this case.

II

In Russia, as everywhere else throughout Europe and America during the early years of the twentieth century, Freud's psycho-analytical doctrine generated intense interest. The Freudian texts were translated into Russian; Russian commentaries burgeoned and proliferated; and Russian disciples set up practice.[16] Naturally, and again as everywhere else, this ferment of interest included the polemics of pro and con forces.

By no means did this activity cease or slacken with the advent of the Soviet regime. But the situation, especially in the latter half of the 1920s, acquired a new and urgent note: a number of eminent Soviet scientists not only expressed approval for at least the "scientific core" of psychoanalysis but even advanced the notion that it— that "scientific core"—"best corresponded to those requirements which Marxism makes incumbent upon a science of psychology." Such a claim aroused considerable and heated controversy, and energetic counterarguments on the part of Marxist spokesmen were not long in coming. One of those counterarguments that set out to prove Freudianism "totally unacceptable from an objective-materialistic point of view" was the book presented here in English translation, *Freudianism: A Critical Sketch* by V. N. Vološinov.[17]

Actually, *Freudianism* was the second such attempt by the same author. Two years earlier, in 1925, an article attacking Freud's psychoanalytical doctrine and contesting its suitability for a Marxist science of psychology had appeared under the byline V. Vološinov in the fifth issue for that year of the journal *Zvezda*, entitled "Po tu storonu social'nogo (o frejdizme)" [Beyond the Social (Concerning Freudianism)] (pp. 186–214). Investigation of the relationship between the two texts has revealed that a large part—approximately three quarters—of the earlier article was incorporated into the later book either verbatim or in versions revised to one or another degree. However, despite their considerable overlap, the most curious and even astounding aspect of the interrelationship between the two texts was their *difference* (aside, of course, from the mere difference in length). This difference consists in the following extraordinary fact: while virtually all other points of attack against Freudianism are represented in "Beyond the Social," that article is completely devoid of any *theory of discourse*, any orientation toward the *problem of language*—devoid, in other words, of precisely that which constitutes the governing principles and the main line of the argument of the book *Freudianism*. For instance, the concept of "verbal reactions," which *Freudianism*'s author expounds in the second chapter of Part I of the book and which he implements throughout his critique of the Freudian psychoanalytical doctrine, has no counterpart in the article whatsoever.[18] Thus, the book, as compared with the article, contains a wholly new epistemological dimension.

However, it is not only to the critical aspect of both works that this difference applies; there is also the *positive* side of the matter. Whereas the author of the book, *Freudianism*, sketches out what, in his opinion, an objective and scientific Marxist psychology should be, basing himself precisely on his theory of discourse (particularly in Chapters 8 and 9 of Part III), the author of the article, "Beyond the Social," had brought to bear a positive view of a Marxist psychology utterly different in character. For the author of the article, the foundations and the direction of development for a Marxist science of psychology had been furnished by the investigation of *reflexes* by I. P. Pavlov and Jacques Loeb's theory of *tropisms;* that is to say, he favored a thoroughly physio-chemical materialist basis for psychology. Adumbrating a positive alternative to the unacceptable Freudian conception of the "unconscious," the author of the article argues:

> By the unconscious we can legitimately understand only some *effect-producing activity*, an energy or force (possibly psychical but equally possibly somatic in nature) that, once having emerged into consciousness—and only in and for the consciousness—acquires those forms and that content (perhaps obscure for the self-observing subject and more distinct for the interpreting analyst) which Freudianism without a qualm then *projects* into its so-called "unconscious" [. . .]
>
> We believe that only a supposition of the sort we are postulating constitutes that essential minimum of hypothesis which adequately explains all the real empirical facts of human behavior that Freud and his disciples have come up with. And, of course, a science can admit only a minimum of hypothesis.
>
> How are we to conceive of this "effect-producing activity" that corresponds to the Freudian unconscious?
>
> Isn't there a risk of our falling out of the frying pan into the fire and coming up ourselves with an even more horrendous metaphysical substance to replace Freud's "id"?
>
> The reader can rest easy on this point. We have no inclination even to suppose some psychical energy in undifferentiated form; we believe that what is involved here are mechanisms of the same sort as have become familiar to us under the name of *reflexes* (Pavlov and his school), in part also *tropisms* (J. Loeb) and other chemisms—in short, processes of a purely somatic and material kind. In any case, it is only on this plane that scientific definitions of Freud's unconscious phenomena might be located. We are of course as yet unable to translate them into the language of scientific materialism, but we

do know, at any rate, the direction in which such a translation could be made possible. (p. 203)

The author of *Freudianism*, too, mentions Pavlov and Loeb but with an amazingly different assessment of the contribution their investigations make to the science of psychology: ". . . when it comes to an explanation of human behavior all this [reflexology, tropisms, and so forth] supplies us very little [. . .] What we call 'the human psyche' and 'consciousness' reflects the dialectics of history to a much greater degree than the dialectics of nature [p. 83 of this book]." Indeed, at an earlier point in his exposition, the author warned of a "serious danger" that threatened objective psychology: "the danger of falling into *naive, mechanistic materialism.*" He notes that this is a danger for biology as well as for psychology, in particular, and he mentions that just such a "primitive materialism" is already "detectable among the American behaviorists and the Russian reflexologists [p. 23 of this book]."[19]

Meanwhile, almost exactly one year after the publication of "Beyond the Social," on the pages of the same journal *Zvezda* (No. 6, 1926, pp. 244–67) appeared another article signed by the same V.N. Vološinov. This article, entitled "Slovo v žizni i slovo v poèzii (k voprosam sociologičeskoj poètiki)" [Word in Life and Word in Poetry (Regarding Questions of Sociological Poetics)],[20] emphatically identified the author's cardinal orientation toward language, toward verbal discourse, or, literally translated from the Russian, "the word," as the key to the study of all—in the author's Marxist usage of the term—"ideological" formations in human life and culture. The basic concepts that were to produce the astonishing epistemological transformation of the author's critique of Freudianism were distinctly registered here: the intrinsically and inalienably *social* nature of language; the implementation of the communication model of addresser-message-addressee (in Vološinov's terms, speaker-hero-listener); the identification of internal and external speech as forms of one and the same phenomenon; the postulation of the "utterance," the speech act, permeated through and through with "social evaluation," as the real unit of human language; the notion of the unity of all "ideological" activity—the single ontological chain from the most inchoate apprehensions on the lowest levels of "behavioral ideology" to fully fledged, complex, and elaborate formations in law, art, religion, government, and so forth.

Precisely those ideas, explicitly formulated for the first time in "Word in Life and Word in Poetry," were utilized and further developed not only in *Freudianism* but also in *Marxism and the Philosophy of Language*, which, in turn, supplied the new dimension of a theory of signs, and all the later articles published by Vološinov. The similarity of those ideas to the ones governing the positive argument (the argument for a sociological poetics) in P. N. Medvedev's *Formal'nyj metod v literaturovedenii (kritičeskoe vvedenie v sociologičeskuju poètiku)* [The Formal Method in the Study of Literature (A Critical Introduction to Sociological Poetics)] (Leningrad, 1928)[21] is patent and substantial; their overlap with certain ideas in Baxtin's 1929 book on Dostoevskij (especially the chapter "Tipy prozaičeskogo slova. Slovo u Dostoevskogo" [Word Types in Prose. Word in Dostoevskij]) is also beyond any doubt. Indeed, these very ideas have been registered among the fundamental ideas of that now internationally acclaimed system of ideas for which it is common practice today, as discussed above, to assign the credit solely to M. M. Baxtin.

III

In his masterwork of 1929, *Marxism and the Philosophy of Language*, Vološinov referred to his earlier study of Freud—the book *Freudianism: A Critical Sketch*—as a "popular" work, one presumably meant for the public at large and not merely for an audience of sophisticates or specialists. This characterization is somewhat misleading, however. That Vološinov operated with a much more complex, perhaps even devious, sense of his "listener," his addressee, is borne out, for instance, by the curious fact that the very same reader for whom the author feels obliged to gloss words such as *amnesia, uterus, penis, bisexual,* and the like is at the same time supposed to be able to take in, without the help of identification or explanatory notes, references to Kant, Spengler, Nietzsche, and even J.-C. Tetens. This peculiar duplexity of addressee has its effect on the style of the work, a style that is at once pedagogical and peripatetic, so to speak. Although all the glosses of words which the original contained have been omitted from the present English translation, the reader will still no doubt be struck by this ambiguity in the relationship between the author and his audience—in itself a topic of special interest to Vološinov and one to which he devoted fundamental attention in *Marxism and the Philosophy of Language* and other writings. This and other, doubtlessly related, features of Vološinov's style—his peculiar "rhetorical" paragraphing, his repetitions of terms with different "tonality," his frequent recourse to conative and phatic signals (*of course, you see, to be sure,* and the like) have been preserved in translation.

The first appearance of the present English translation (New York, San Francisco, London: Academic Press, 1976) was given the title *Freudianism: A Marxist Critique,* whereas in actual fact the word "Marxist" does not figure in the original Russian title. The addition of the word "Marxist" seemed justified, since for the Soviet readers of the original book the Marxist nature of the critique was an automatic assumption on which the author could rely, but no such assumption applied, of course, to Western readers. To deny the validity of adding the word "Marxist" to the title, as has been done since the first appearance of this translation, is to ignore the author's own explicit and repeated declarations that his critique is Marxist and is meant to serve the interests of a specifically Marxist conception of psychology. When the author says such things as ". . . we consider it essential, before presenting an exposition of psychoanalysis, to provide the reader an introduction on the topic of the basic trends in modern psychology and, moreover, to make him aware of what the Marxist point of view might well demand in regard to the methodological bases of this science [p. 17 of this book]," or "Which of [the two trends in modern psychology—subjective and objective] is in closer correspondence to the basic principles of dialectical materialism? Of course, it is the second, the objective trend in psychology. It alone answers the requirements of *materialistic monism* [p. 21]," or when the author appeals to the "objective-sociological methods that Marxism has worked out for the analysis of various ideological systems" for help in reaching "the objective roots" of human behavior [p. 87], aren't we obliged to take him at his word? I thought, and still think, that we are, whether or not we sympathize with the author's overt point of view. However, in consideration of the fact that there is a controversy about the matter, as already discussed in the first part of this Introduction, and, moreover, at the express request of Indiana University Press, this reprint of the translation is being published under a strictly literal rendition of the original Russian title.

A curious feature of the original text is the appearance from time to time, in the course of the first several chapters, of footnotes with the designation *"Prim. red.,"* that is, comment by an editor. The identity of this "editor" is nowhere disclosed. The comments themselves are almost exclusively of the informational variety and clearly date from the year of publication, 1927 (the text and the author's own footnotes never make reference to works published in 1927, suggesting that the manuscript had been prepared and submitted for publication the year before). All the comments in question have been retained in the translation and are labeled "Editor's note."

The omission in the first publication of this translation of a number of the original footnotes, consisting merely of references to Russian translations of works by Freud and others, has been carried over to this publication as well. However, the deletion from the earlier publication of the final (tenth) chapter of the original book, where the author presents his refutation of specific pro-Freudian arguments on the part of four Soviet psychologists (the deletion having been motivated by the presumed parochialism of those concerns), has been rectified in the present publication with the addition of a translation of that chapter by Liv Tudge, reprinted from *Soviet Psychology*, Vol. 23, no. 3, spring 1985, by permission of M. E. Sharpe, Inc. Indiana University Press has chosen to reprint the translation of chapter 10 without adjusting its transliteration and terminology to conform to those used in the rest of the translation; however, errors of translation have been corrected.

Certain typographical and other minor errors in the translated text of the Academic Press edition have been corrected. The introductions and afterword printed in that edition have been substantially revised and updated for this Indiana University Press edition and a foreword by James V. Wertsch has been added.

Finally, the translator gratefully acknowledges his considerable debt to the coeditor of this volume, Neal H. Bruss, for having read the entire manuscript of the translation (Chapters 1–9) and made numerous helpful suggestions. Thanks are also due Bruce Kochis and especially Beth Forer for their generous help in doing library research.

I. R. TITUNIK

Notes

1. I have in mind here specifically the so-called "disputed works"—a matter about which the uninitiated reader will shortly be informed in what follows. In their book, *Mikhail Bakhtin* (Cambridge, Mass., and London: Harvard University Press, 1984), where the "disputed works"

are all assigned to M. M. Baxtin, Katerina Clark and Michael Holquist do mention a number of other, *undisputed* works by Vološinov (essays, reviews, and poems). There, too, the reader will find such information as is currently available about the life and career of V. N. Vološinov (see especially pp. 39–40, 49, 110–11, 117, and 265).

2. See L. Matejka, "The Roots of Russian Semiotics of Art," *The Sign (Semiotics Around the World)*, edited by R. W. Bailey, L. Matejka, and P. Steiner, Ann Arbor, 1978, pp. 167–68.

3. First published in 1957 by the Harvard University Department of Slavic Languages and Literatures.

4. *Marxism and the Philosophy of Language*, translated by Ladislav Matejka and I. R. Titunik, Seminar Press, New York and London, 1973. This was the first translation into any language not only of that particular book but also of any of the writings of V. N. Vološinov. A reprint of the translation, with an added "Translators' Preface 1986," has been issued by Harvard University Press, 1986.

5. *Problemy tvorčestva Dostoevskogo* [Problems of Dostoevskij's Creative Art], Leningrad, 1929.

6. *Problemy poètiki Dostoevskogo* [Problems of Dostoevskij's Poetics], Moscow, 1963, and *Tvorčestvo Fransua Rable i narodnaja kul'tura Srednevekov'ja i Renesansa* [The Creative Art of François Rabelais and the Popular Culture of the Middle Ages and the Renaissance], Moscow, 1965. Both books have been translated into English and several other languages.

7. "Značenie idej M. M. Baxtina o znake, vyskazyvanii i dialoge dlja sovremennoj semiotiki" [The Significance of M. M. Baxtin's Ideas on Sign, Utterance, and Dialogue for Modern Semiotics], *Trudy po znakovym sistemam*, 6, Tartu, 1973, p. 44. An English translation of this article appears in *Semiotics and Structuralism (Readings from the Soviet Union)*, edited by H. Baran, International Arts and Sciences Press, White Plains, New York, 1976, pp. 310–67.

8. I must add here that the much touted *glasnost'* of the current regime in the Soviet Union has, as of the moment of this writing and to the best of my knowledge, had no effect whatsoever in the area of concern here. A particularly striking—and distressing—sign of no change is provided by a 1985 collection of essays published by Baxtin's disciples in Saransk (where he spent so many of his later years) under the title: *Problemy naučnogo nasledija M. M. Baxtina* [Problems of M. M. Baxtin's Scholarly Legacy]. While kudos are paid to "Comrade M. S. Gorbačev" in the preface signed by the editorial board of the collection, not so much as a single glimmer of new light is shed; indeed, if anything, obfuscation is produced. In the "Critico-biographical sketch of Mixail Baxtin," which opens the collection and which was written by its chief editor, S. S. Konkin, we are treated to banal thumb-nail descriptions of the lives of V. N. Vološinov and P. N. Medvedev during the years 1919–1924 (and *only* during those years), whereupon the author appends the comment: "Such were the people with whom, during the years 1919–1929 [*Nota Bene!* IRT], M. Baxtin shared the joys of whole-hearted engagement in cultural-educational (in Vitebsk especially) and scholarly activities, helping them advance to the leading edge of scientific inquiry of the day." (p. 10) Not one single further word about the matter is said in the entire body of the text of that sketch. Only in an appended note (number 12, p. 23) does S. S. Konkin inform the reader about the attribution to Baxtin of "the basic text of works published in the 1920s under the names of V. N. Vološinov and P. N. Medvedev," citing as proof—and the only proof—of this contention V. V. Ivanov's original statement of 1973!

9. A certain amount of commentary and argument on the subject has developed over the last decade or so. Several of the contributions to the discussion will be mentioned in what follows. I have had my own say at length on the matter in my article "Baxtin &/or Vološinov &/or Medvedev: Dialogue &/or Doubletalk?," *Language and Literary Theory*, edited by B. Stolz et al., Papers in Slavic Philology 5, Ann Arbor, 1984, pp. 535–64 (selected bibliography included).

10. See his "The Politics of Representation," *Allegory and Representation*, edited by S. J. Greenblatt, Selected Papers from the English Institute 5, Baltimore, 1979–80, and (with Katerina Clark) *Mikhail Bakhtin* (see note 1 above).

11. Pavel Medvedev, *Die formale Methode in der Literaturwissenschaft*, translated and edited by Helmut Glück, Stuttgart, 1976 (see Glück's introduction, especially pp. xx–xxi).

12. Mikhail Bakhtine (V. N. Vološinov), *Le Marxisme et la philosophie du langage*, translated and presented by M. Yaguello with a preface by Roman Jakobson, Paris, 1977 (see Yaguello's introduction, especially pp. 11–12); Mihail Bahtin, *Marksizam i filozofija jezika*, translated by Radovan Matijašević, Belgrade, 1980 (see Matijašević's introduction, especially p. xiv); Frederic Jameson, review of *Marxism and the Philosophy of Language* in *Style*, 3, Fall 1974, pp. 535–45.

13. Tzvetan Todorov, *Mikhail Bakhtine: Le principe dialogique, suivi de Écrits du Cercle de Bakhtine*, Paris, 1981 (see especially pp. 20–21).

14. A point already made by V. V. Ivanov in his celebratory address (see the work cited in note 7 above, p. 30).

15. See my article cited in note 9 above, pp. 540–46.

16. An account (very biased but informative nevertheless) of the Russian and Soviet-Russian interest in Freud is given in A. V. Petrovskij, *Istorija sovetskoj psixologii*, Moscow, 1967, pp. 79–94.

17. On the Soviet controversy over Freud in the 1920s, see Martin A. Miller, "Freudian Theory Under Bolshevik Rule: The Theoretical Controversy During the 1920s," *Slavic Review*, Winter 1985, pp. 624–46. Curiously enough, Miller only mentions Vološinov's *Freudianism* in passing, leaving it entirely out of his discussion of the controversy, and no mention at all is made of "Beyond the Social" (about which see below).

18. What is more, Freud's definition of the unconscious as the "non-verbal" was interpreted in the article merely as Freud's effort to compensate somewhat for his otherwise "metaphysical" concept of the unconscious (p. 203).

19. For a detailed comparative analysis of the two texts, see my article cited in note 9 above, pp. 548–60. Precisely what motivated the extraordinary epistemological shift from the position of the article to that of the book is unknown and constitutes a formidable puzzle, whether Vološinov be considered the author of both works or whether both works be attributed to Baxtin (indeed, especially in this case) or even whether the works be somehow distributed between them. Moreover, another piece of the puzzle must also be mentioned here. M. Holquist has claimed that Baxtin is also the author of an article signed by the biologist I. Kanaev, "Sovremennyj vitalizm" [Contemporary Vitalism], *Čelovek i Priroda*, 1926, No. 1:33–42 and No. 2:9–22. The author of this article sets out to prove as something unscientific and absurd the subjective-idealist conception of biology expounded by the neo-vitalist Hans Driesch and to refute Driesch's proof that the mechanistic-materialist conception of biology is unscientific and absurd. If Baxtin was its author, as alleged, then once again he acquires a new style and a new technical register (that of the professional biologist) and, what is more, the contradiction in views noted above is further ramified: in 1925 Baxtin approves the mechanistic-materialist foundation of psychology ("Beyond the Social") and the very next year he first approves the mechanistic-materialist foundation of biology ("Contemporary Vitalism") and then rejects the mechanistic-materialist foundation of both biology and psychology (*Freudianism*) . . . and all in the interests of Marxist science!

20. My translation of this article under the title "Discourse in Life and Discourse in Art" is presented on pp. 93–116 of this book. The author of *Freudianism* makes special mention of the article in Chapter 8 (see p. 79 of this book).

21. English translation by Albert J. Wehrle, with the author designated as M. M. Bakhtin/P. N. Medvedev, *The Formal Method in Literary Scholarship: A Critical Introduction to Sociological Poetics*, Baltimore and London: Johns Hopkins University Press, 1978; reprint, Cambridge, MA: Harvard University Press, 1985.

Guide to Transliteration

Russian names and words in the translated text and footnotes and in the appendices are transliterated in accordance with the standard scholarly system in which the following special signs have the approximate values indicated below:

'   *soft sign*, indicating that the preceding consonant is "softened" (i.e., palatalized)

"   *hard sign*, indicating that the preceding consonant is not palatalized

c   *ts*

č   *ch*

e   *e*, as in *egg*

e   *e*, as in *egg*, preceded by "j" as explained below

j   *y* initially (before a vowel), terminally (after a vowel), medially between vowels or between hard or soft sign and a vowel; elsewhere indicates that the preceding consonant is palatalized

š   *sh*

šč *shch*

x   *h*

y   *i*, as in *bill*

ž   *zh*

Compare the following examples of certain Russian names in their common English spellings and their transliterated equivalents: Chekhov = Čexov, Dostoyevsky = Dostoevskij, Gogol = Gogol', Pushkin = Puškin, Tolstoy = Tolstoj, etc.

FREUDIANISM
A Marxist Critique

PART I

FREUDIANISM AND MODERN TRENDS
IN PHILOSOPHY AND PSYCHOLOGY
(CRITICAL ORIENTATION)

CHAPTER 1

The Basic Ideological Motif
of Freudianism

*Freudianism and the modern world. The ideological motif of
Freudianism. Similar motifs in modern philosophy. A preliminary evaluation of Freudianism.*

In 1893 a short article by two Viennese doctors, Freud and Breuer, appeared
on the pages of a professional journal of psychiatry.[1] The article, devoted to a
new method of treating hysteria through the use of hypnosis, was entitled by its
authors "On the Psychical Mechanism of Hysterical Phenomena (Preliminary
Communication)." From the kernel of this "preliminary communication" was to
develop one of the most popular ideological trends in modern Europe—psychoanalysis.

Inaugurated as a *modest psychiatric method*[2] with a barely developed
theoretical basis, psychoanalysis had, by the end of its first decade of existence,
already devised a *general theory of psychology* of its own that cast a new light
on all aspects of the mental life of man. Thereupon, work was undertaken to
apply this new psychological theory to the task of elucidating various domains
of cultural creativity—art, religion, and, finally, aspects of social and political
life. Thus, psychoanalysis succeeded in elaborating its own *philosophy of
culture*. These later postulations of psychoanalysis in general psychology and
philosophy gradually came to overshadow the original, purely psychiatric core of
the doctrine.[3]

[1] This article was later included in the book by J. Breuer and S. Freud, *Studien über
Hysterie* (1895; 4th ed., 1922).
[2] The method that Freud and Breuer proposed for treating hysteria was meant only to
supplement other methods already in medical use.
[3] Not all psychoanalysts would agree with this assertion, but it is true, nevertheless.
Freud's two recent books, *Jenseits des Lustprincips* (1920) and *Das Ich und Das Es* (1923),

Psychoanalysis achieved success among wide circles of the European intelligentsia even before World War I. After the war, and especially in recent years [the late 1920s], its influence reached extraordinary proportions in all the countries of Europe and in America. Owing to the breadth of this influence in the bourgeois world and among intellectual circles, psychoanalysis advanced to a position far beyond other contemporary ideological movements; Steiner's "anthroposophy" alone was possibly able to compete with it. Even such fashionable trends of the past as Bergsonism and Nietzscheanism had never, even at the height of their success, rallied so huge a body of supporters and "interested persons" as Freudianism.

The comparatively slow and, at first (up to 1910 approximately), very difficult progress of psychoanalysis en route to its "conquest of Europe" attests to the fact that this movement was no momentary and superficial "mode of the day," in the style of Spenglerism, but rather an abiding and profound expression of certain crucial aspects of European bourgeois reality. Therefore, *anyone wishing to fathom the spiritual physiognomy of modern Europe can hardly bypass psychoanalysis; it has become too signal and too indelible a feature of modern times.*[4]

How is the success of psychoanalysis to be explained? What is its attraction for a member of the European bourgeoisie?

Needless to say, it is not the specifically scientific, psychiatric aspect of the doctrine. It would be naive to suppose that masses of ardent devotees came to psychoanalysis through interest in the technical problems of psychiatry and through acquaintance with the professional publications in the field. That was not the way they encountered Freudianism. In the vast majority of cases, Freud was the first and last psychiatrist they read and *Internationale Zeitschrift für Psychoanalyse* the first and only professional journal of psychology whose pages they opened. It would be naive to suppose that Freud had somehow managed to engage the attention of vast circles of people to the technical issues of

---

are purely philsosophical in character. At the most recent International Congress of Psychoanalysts, in 1922, a great many participants expressed the apprehension that the speculative side of psychoanalysis had thoroughly overshadowed its original therapeutic purpose. On 'this point, see S. Ferenczi and O. Rank, *Entwicklungsziele der Psychoanalyse* (1924).

[4] One can judge how widespread the Freudian movement has become by the fact that there is now an entire international organization of Freudians. The Eighth Congress of Freudians was held in 1924 and was attended by representatives from various local groups in Vienna, Budapest, Berlin, Holland, Zurich, London, New York, Calcutta, and Moscow. There are now several periodical publications devoted to psychoanalysis and a special publishing house—the International Psychoanalytical Press in Budapest. The first psychoanalytical clinic for the indigent mentally ill was opened in Berlin in 1920.

psychiatry. Obviously, neither was it practical interest in the achievements of a therapeutic method that made psychoanalysis attractive. It would be absurd to assume that all those masses of Freud's devotees were and are patients at psychiatric clinics eager for a cure. It is beyond doubt that Freud did succeed in striking a nerve in the modern bourgeoisie, but not through the specifically scientific or narrowly practical aspects of his doctrine.

Any ideological movement that is not the restricted property of some select group of specialists but encompasses wide and varied masses of readers who are obviously incapable of coping with the technical details and subtleties of the doctrine—any such ideological movement always allows of definition in terms of a *certain basic motif*, the *ideological dominant* of the whole system that determines its success and influence. This basic motif possesses a power of conviction and revelation all of its own and is relatively independent of the complex apparatus of its scientific foundation, to which the public at large does not have access. Therefore, this basic motif can be isolated and formulated in a rough and simple way without the risk of doing an injustice.

In this first—introductory—chapter we intend, somewhat anticipating our later exposition, to take up the task of singling out the basic ideological motif of Freudianism and providing preliminary evaluation of it.

We are guided in doing this by the following considerations.

Before the reader can be introduced into the rather complex and, at times, alluring labyrinth of the psychoanalytical doctrine, he needs to have a solid critical orientation given him. We must first of all show the reader in what philosophical context, that is, in line with which other philosophical currents that have held sway or still do hold sway over the minds of the European intelligentsia, he must perceive psychoanalysis so as to obtain an accurate notion of its ideological essence and value. That is the reason why it is necessary to feature the basic ideological motif of psychoanalysis. We shall see that this motif is by no means anything totally new or surprising, but rather that it is something that can be completely accommodated within the mainstream of all the ideological tendencies of bourgeois philosophy in the first quarter of the twentieth century—perhaps, indeed, the most striking and daring expression of those tendencies.

In the following chapter (Chapter 2), we shall endeavor to give the reader a similar critical orientation for viewing the purely psychological aspect of the Freudian doctrine, without as yet fully expositing that doctrine itself but acquainting the reader with the rivalry of various different trends in modern psychology. In this way we shall define the context within which the specifically psychological tenets of Freudianism should be viewed and judged.

Once the reader has been critically armed and made aware of the historical perspectives in which to view this new phenomenon, we shall proceed, starting with the third chapter, to a systematic exposition of psychoanalysis without recourse to critical commentary. In Part III of our study we shall return again to the critical themes noted in the first two chapters of Part I.

What, then, is the basic ideological motif of Freudianism?

A human being's fate, the whole content of his life and creative activity—of his art, if he is an artist, of his scientific theories, if he is a scientist, of his political programs and measures, if he is a politician, and so on—are wholly and exclusively determined by the vicissitudes of his sexual instinct. Everything else represents merely the overtones of the mighty and fundamental melody of sex.[5]

If a person's consciousness tells him otherwise about the motives and driving forces of his life and creativity, then that consciousness is lying. A *skeptical attitude toward consciousness* is an ever-present accompaniment to the development of Freud's basic theme.

Thus, what really counts in a human being is not at all what determines *his place and role in history*—the *class, nation, historical period* to which he belongs; only his *sex* and his *age* are essential, everything else being merely a superstructure. *A person's consciousness is shaped not by his historical existence but by his biological being,* the main facet of which is *sexuality.*

Such is the basic ideological motif of Freudianism.

In its general form this motif is nothing new and original. What is new and original is the elaboration of its component parts—the *concepts of sex and age.* In this respect Freud did genuinely succeed in disclosing an enormous wealth and variety of new factors and subtleties that had never before been submitted to scientific inquiry, owing to the monstrous hypocrisy of official science in all questions having to do with human sexual life. Freud so expanded and so enriched the concept of sexuality that the notions we ordinarily associate with that concept comprise merely a tiny sector of its vast territory. This must be kept in mind when making judgements about psychoanalysis. One ought not lose sight of this new and extremely expanded meaning of the term "sexual" in Freud, when, for instance, accusing psychoanalysis, as is commonly done, of "pansexualism."

Psychoanalysis has, furthermore, revealed much that is surprising also in the matter of the connection between sex and age. The history of a human being's sexual drive starts at the moment of his birth and proceeds to pass through a long series of individually marked stages of development that by no means correspond to the naive scheme of "innocent childhood-puberty-innocent old

---

[5] The author here emphasizes only the *basic* motif of Freudianism. From his later exposition (Chapter 3), the reader will learn that the doctrine on the existence of unconscious mental processes and on "resistance" and "repression" are equally integral parts of Freudianism (see Freud's article, "Psychoanalyse," in *Handwörterbuch der Sexualwissenschaft*, ed. M. Marcuse (Bonn, 1926), p. 614). [*Editor's note*]

age." The riddle about the ages of man that the Sphinx asked Oedipus found in Freud a unique and surprising solution. How sound a solution is another matter, one we shall take up later on. Here we need only note that *both component parts of the basic ideological motif of Freudianism—sex and age—are invested with thoroughly new and rich content.* That is why this motif, old in and of itself, has a new ring to it.

It is an old motif. It is constantly repeated during all those periods in the development of mankind when the social groups and classes that had been the makers of history are in process of being replaced. It is the *leitmotif of crisis and decline.*

Whenever such a social class finds itself in a state of disintegration and is compelled to retreat from the arena of history, its ideology begins insistently to harp on one theme, which it repeats in every possible variation: *Man is above all an animal.* And from the vantage point of this "revelation" it strives to put a new construction on all the values that make up history and the world. Meanwhile, the second part of Aristotle's famous formula—"man is a *social* animal"—is totally ignored.

The ideology of periods such as these shifts its center of gravity onto the isolated biological organism; the three basic events in the life of all animals—birth, copulation, and death—begin to compete with historical events in terms of ideological significance and, as it were, become a surrogate of history.

That which in man is nonsocial and nonhistorical is abstracted and advanced to the position of the ultimate measure and criterion for all that is social and historical. It is almost as if people of such periods desire to leave the atmosphere of history, which has become too cold and comfortless, and take refuge in the organic warmth of the animal side of life.

That is what happened during the period of the break-up of the Greek city states, during the decline of the Roman Empire, during the period of the disintegration of the feudal-aristocratic order before the French Revolution.

The motif of the *supreme power and wisdom of Nature* (above all, of man's nature—his biological drives) and of the *impotence of history with its much ado about nothing*—this motif equally resounds, despite differences of nuance and variety of emotional register, in such phenomena as epicureanism, stoicism, the literature of the Roman decadence (e.g. Petronius' *Satyricon*), the skeptical ratiocination of the French aristocrats in the seventeenth and early eighteenth centuries. *A fear of history, a shift in orientation toward the values of personal, private life, the primacy of the biological and the sexual in man*—such are the features common to all of these ideological phenomena.

And now once again, starting at the very end of the nineteenth century, motifs of the same kind have been distinctly voiced in European ideology. For twentieth century bourgeois philosophy the abstract biological organism has again become the central hero.

The philosophy of "Pure Reason" (Kant), of the "Creative I" (Fichte), of "Idea and the Absolute Spirit" (Hegel), that is, that which constituted the undeniably energetic and, in its way, respectable philosophy of the heroic age of the bourgeoisie (end of the eighteenth and first half of the nineteenth century), such philosophy still commanded a full measure of enthusiasm for history and organization (in the bourgeois style). In the second half of the nineteenth century this philosophy became increasingly diminished and gradually came to a standstill in the lifeless and static schemes of the "school philosophy" of epigones (neo-Kantians, neo-Fichteans, neo-Hegelians), finally to be replaced in our time by the passive and flabby "Philosophy of Life" with its biologistic and psychologistic coloration and its implementation of every possible shade of meaning and combination of the verb "to live."[6]

The biological terms for the various organic processes have literally deluged the modern Weltanschauung: Efforts are made to find biological metaphors for everything, so as to impart an agreeable animation to whatever the cold of Kantian Pure Reason had benumbed.

What are the basic features of this philosophy of the present day?

All thinkers of modern times, such as Bergson, Simmel, Gomperz, the pragmatists, Scheler, Driesch, Spengler, despite the many points and ways wherein they disagree with one another, are fundamentally united under the headings of three motifs:

1. *Life in the biological sense stands at the center of the philosophical system.* Isolated organic unity is declared to be the highest value and criterion of philosophy.

2. *Distrust of consciousness.* The attempt is made to minimize the role of consciousness in cultural creativity. Hence the criticism of the Kantian doctrine as a philosophy of consciousness.

3. *The attempt is made to replace all objective socioeconomic categories with subjective psychological or biological ones.* This explains a tendency to view history and culture as deriving directly from nature and to disregard economics.

Thus, Bergson, who still remains one of the most popular of European philosophers, posited at the center of his entire philosophical system the concept of a single *life force*—the *élan vital*, from which he endeavored to derive all forms of cultural activity. The higher forms of cognition (specifically, intuitive philosophical cognition) and artistic creativity were brought in line with *instinct*, which most fully expressed the unity of the continuum of life. The intellect, the creator of the positive sciences, was treated by Bergson with disdain, but

---

[6] See H. Rickert, *Die Philosophie des Lebens*. The book contains a good deal of information, but the author's point of view—that of an idealist-neo-Kantian—is unacceptable.

nevertheless he derived its forms also directly from the biological structure of the organism.[7]

The late Georg Simmel—a Kantian in his earliest works—became one of the twentieth century's most impressive exponents of fashionable biological tendencies. The *enclosed organic unity of individual life* came to stand for him as the highest criterion of all cultural values. Sense and meaning accrue only to those things that can be attached to that self-sufficient unity. In one of his fundamental works, *Individual Law*, Simmel endeavored to conceptualize ethical law as the law of the individual development of personhood. Taking issue with Kant, who required that ethical law have the form of *universality* (the categorical imperative), Simmel developed his own notion of an individual ethical law that is supposed to regulate not the relations of human beings in society but the relations of forces and drives within the enclosed and self-sufficient organism.[8]

The biologistic bent in philosophy has taken even cruder forms in the work of the pragmatists. Adherents of the late American psychologist William James, the father of the pragmatist movement, these people strive to reduce all types of cultural creativity to the biological processes of adaptation, expediency, and so on.[9]

A close resemblance of sorts to Freudianism is exhibited by the never-completed philosophical system of Freud's compatriot, the Viennese philosopher Heinrich Gomperz, called "Pathemperism." Gomperz attempted to reduce all categories of thought—causality, object, and so on—to feelings, to the emotional reactions of the human organism to the world. The influence of the Viennese sexologist, Otto Weininger, is detectable here.[10]

We find the same motifs, although in a considerably more complex form, in the thought of the most influential German philosopher of our day, Max Scheler, the chief representative of the phenomenological school. Scheler combines together the struggle against psychologism and primitive biologism and, thus, the advocacy of objectivism, on the one hand, with deep distrust of consciousness and its forms and, thus, preference for intuitive modes of cognition, on the other. All positive, empirical sciences Scheler, in this respect

[7] Bergson's most important philosophical work is *L'Evolution Créatrice*.

[8] See Simmel, "Das individuelle Gesetz: Ein Versuch über das Prinzip der Ethik," *Logos* 4 (1913): 117-160. This work later appeared as a chapter in Simmel's last book, *Lebensanschauung* (1919). On Simmel, the Russian reader is referred to a brief article of Marxist orientation by Svjatlovskij appended to the translation of Simmel's *Conflicts of Modern Culture*—"Konflikty sovremennoj kul'tury," *Načatki znanij* (Petrograd, 1923).

[9] See James, *Pragmatism*, which is the basic philosphical work of the pragmatist movement.

[10] Gomperz's basic work is *Anschauungslehre*. Regarding Weininger's influence on him, see the Russian translation, *Učenie o mirovozzrenii* (Šipovnik Publishing House), pp. 172-175.

joining Bergson, derives from the forms of the biological organism's adaptation to the world.[11]

The ambition to subordinate philosophy to the needs and methods of the particular discipline of biology is most consistently expressed in the philosophical works of Hans Driesch, the well-known biologist-neovitalist, one of the founders of experimental morphology, who now occupies a chair of philosophy. The basic concept in his system is termed "entelechy," after Aristotle. Entelechy is supposedly the quintessence of organic unity and functionality. It governs all manifestations of the organism, its highest cultural activity as well as its lowest biological functions.[12]

Finally, let us make mention of the once-upon-a-time renowned but now almost forgotten attempt of Spengler to apply biological categories to the interpretation of the historical process.[13]

Thus, we see that the basic ideological motif of Freudianism is by no means its motif alone. The motif chimes in unison with all the basic motifs of contemporary bourgeois philosophy. *A sui generis fear of history, an ambition to locate a world beyond the social and the historical, a search for this world precisely in the depths of the organic—these are the features that pervade all systems of contemporary philosophy and constitute the symptom of the disintegration and decline of the bourgeois world.*

Freud's notion of the "sexual" is the extreme pole of this fashionable biologism. It gathers and concentrates in one compact and piquant image all the separate elements of modern-day antihistoricism.

What should be our attitude toward the basic theme of contemporary philosophy? Is there any substance to the attempt to derive all cultural creativity from the biological roots of the human organism?

---

[11] Among M. Scheler's works we shall name here only *Phenomenologie und Theorie der Sympathiegefühle* (Halle, 1913) and *Vom Ewigen im Menschen* (1920). There are no Russian works on Scheler with the exception of an article by Bammel', "Maks Šeler, katolicizm i rabočee diviženie" [Max Scheler, Catholicism and the Workers' Movement], *Pod znamenem Marksizma*, 7-8 (1926). A separate chapter is devoted to Scheler in our book, now being prepared for publication, *Filosofičeskaja mysl' sovremennogo Zapada* [Philosphical Thought in the West Today (there is no evidence that this book was ever actually published. *Translator*)]. A few pages of analysis and evaluation of Freudianism are included in the first of Scheler's works cited above.

[12] Driesch's basic work is: *Philosophie des Organischen*, 2 vols. (1909, one-volume ed., 1921). Others are: *Ordnungslehre* (1926), *Wirklichkeitslehre* (1924), and *Der Vitalismus als Geschichte und als Lehre* (1905). Among Russian works on Driesch, see N. I. Kanaev, "Sovremennyj vitalizm" [Contemporary Vitalism], in *Čelovek i Priroda*, (Nos. 1-2, 1926).

[13] *Untergang des Abendlandes*, 2 vols. Marxist criticism of Spengler can be found in: Deborin, "Gibel' Evropy, ili toržestvo imperializma [The End of Europe or the Triumph of Imperialism], in *Filosofija i Marksizm (sbornik statej)* (GIZ, 1926).

The abstract biological person, biological individual—that which has become the alpha and omega of modern ideology—does not exist at all. It is an improper abstraction. Outside society and, consequently, outside objective socioeconomic conditions, there is no such thing as a human being. *Only as a part of a social whole, only in and through a social class, does the human person become historically real and culturally productive.* In order to enter into history it is not enough to be born physically. Animals are physically born but they do not enter into history. What is needed is, as it were, a second birth, a *social* birth. A human being is not born as an abstract biological organism but as a landowner or a peasant, as a bourgeois or a proletarian, and so on—that is the main thing. Furthermore, he is born a Russian or a Frenchman, and he is born in 1800 or 1900, and so on. *Only this social and historical localization makes him a real human being* and determines the content of his life and cultural creativity. All attempts to bypass this second, social, birth and to derive everything from the biological premises of the organism's existence are vain and doomed beforehand to fail. Not a single action taken by a whole person, not a single concrete ideological formation (a thought, an artistic image, even the content of dreams) can be explained and understood without reference to socioeconomic factors. What is more, even the technical problems of biology can never find thoroughgoing solution unless biology takes comprehensive account of the social position of the human organism it studies. After all, "the essence of man is not an abstraction inherent in each separate individual. In its reality it is the aggregate of social relationships."[14]

---

[14] From the *Sixth Thesis on Feuerbach*. [English translation quoted from *The German Ideology* (London: The Marxist-Leninist Library, 1942, vol. 17) p. 198. *Translator.*]

CHAPTER 2

Two Trends
in Modern Psychology

*Formulation of the issue. Experimental psychology. Objective
psychology. Verbal reaction. Marxism and psychology. The
psychological problem of Freudianism. Science and class.*

We are now acquainted with the basic motif of psychoanalysis and have
determined its intimate connection with other modern European ideological
trends. *This motif runs throughout the psychoanalysts' theories at all levels.* Of
course, it finds its clearest, ideologically most patent expression in a special
philosophy of culture, but even within the psychological doctrine, behind the
technical, specifically scientific apparatus of the system, we can discover *exactly
the same motif* functioning as the determinative principle of all of the Freudians'
notions about the mental life of human beings and the forces governing it.

Nevertheless, a fairly widespread opinion has it that, notwithstanding the
faultiness and untenability of its basic ideological motif, psychoanalysis still
does contain a sound, scientifically valuable core, which is, namely, its
psychological theory.[1] Proponents of this point of view maintain that the
technical psychological doctrine of Freud is completely compatible with a
different philosophical outlook and that, as a matter of fact, it best corresponds
to those requirements which Marxism makes incumbent upon a science of
psychology.

It is precisely in order to deal with this issue that we consider it essential,
before presenting an exposition of psychoanalysis, to provide the reader an
introduction on the topic of the basic trends in modern psychology and,
moreover, to make him aware of what the Marxist point of view might well
demand in regard to the methodological bases of this science.

[1] This is the point of view shared by Bykovskij, Zalkind, Fridman, Luria, and others.

17

At the present time, both in Europe and here in the USSR, two trends in the study of the psychical life of humans and animals are engaged in spirited controversy. This is the *controversy between objective and subjective psychology*.

Each of these trends breaks down, in turn, into a series of individually marked tendencies. We shall identify only the most important of these in what follows, without going into the matter of their special and differential features. All that we really need is the basic distinction between the points of view of the subjectivists and the objectivists.

The variant of subjective psychology of most serious interest is Experimental Psychology (Wundt school, James school, and others—its major local representative is Professor Čelpanov), while the variants of objective psychology of similar weight are Reflexology (Pavlov school,[2] Bexterev[3] and others) and the so-called Science of Behavior, or Behaviorism, which is cultivated particularly in America (Watson,[4] Parmelee,[5] Dewey, and others). In the USSR, work in a direction similar to behaviorism is being done by Blonskij and Kornilov (Reactology).[6]

Now, what is the main source of disagreement between subjective and objective psychology?

Psychical life is accessible to human beings in two ways:

1. *Within his own self* a human being directly, through *internal apprehension*, observes the occurrence of various mental experiences—thoughts, feelings, desires.

2. With regard to other people or to animals, he can observe only the *outward expression* of psychical life in terms of the various *reactions* of other organisms to stimuli. For *external apprehension* there are, of course, no such things as desires, feelings, ambitions—after all, they cannot be seen or heard or touched; there are only specific material processes that occur in the reacting organism (i.e., in responding to stimuli). This outward material-corporeal

---

[2] I. P. Pavlov, *25-letnij opyt ob"ektivnogo izučenija vysšej nervnoj dejatel'nosti životnyx* [Twenty-Five Years of Objective Study of the Higher Nervous Activity of Animals] (1926), *Lekcii o rabote bol'šix polušarij golovnogo mozga* [Lectures on the Functioning of the Large Cerebral Hemispheres] (1927).

[3] V. M. Bexterev, *Obščie osnovy refleksologii čeloveka* [General Principles of Human Reflexology] (Petrograd, 1923; 3rd ed., 1926).

[4] J. B. Watson, *Psychology from the Standpoint of a Behaviourist* (London, 1919).

[5] M. Parmelee, *The Science of Human Behavior* (New York, 1921).

[6] Kornilov, *Učenie o reakcijax čeloveka* [Teachings on Human Reactions] (Moscow, 1921; 2nd ed., GIZ, 1927). Also his *Učebnik psixologii, izložennoj s točki zrenija dialektičeskogo materializma* [A Textbook in Psychology from the Standpoint of Dialectical Materialism] (Moscow, 1926).

language of psychical life is, of course, observable by a human being with respect to himself, as well.

The question now is: Which of the two kinds of apprehension—internal-subjective or external-objective—ought to form the basis for a scientific psychology? Or might not some particular combination of the data of both serve that purpose?

We must first remark that no one any longer seriously defends pure subjective apprehension, without any admixture of data supplied by external apprehension, as the exclusive basis of psychology. What representatives of the contemporary version of subjective psychology now assert is that the basis of psychology can be provided only by *direct observation* of mental life (by *introspection*), but that its data must be amplified and controlled by external, objective observation. That is precisely the purpose an experiment serves, that is, an experiment is the deliberate causing of psychical phenomena, psychical experience, under predetermined external conditions erected by the experimenter himself.

This being the case, the makeup of such a psychological experiment is inevitably twofold:

1. One part of it, namely, the entire *external, physical situation* in which the experience under study occurs—the circumstances, the stimulus, the outward corporeal expression of stimulation, and the reaction of the subject—is located *in the field of the experimenter's external, objective apprehension*. This entire part of the experiment is amenable to methods of exact, natural-scientific ascertainment, analysis, and measurement with the help of special instruments.

2. The second part of the experiment—the psychical experience—is not present to the experimenter's external apprehension; indeed, it necessarily lies beyond any apprehension from outside. This part of the experiment is present only to the *internal apprehension* of the subject himself, who, in fact, reports the results of his *self-observation* to the experimenter. The subject's direct, *inner* data are then taken by the experimenter and placed in conjunction with the data of his, the experimenter's, own *external*, objective apprehension.

Clearly, the center of gravity of the whole experiment lies in its second, subjective part, that is, in the subject's inner experience; the experimenter's focus of attention is set precisely on it. This inner experience is, then, in point of fact, what psychology studies.

Thus, *in experimental psychology introspection has the final word*. Everything else, all those instruments for exact measurement, in which representatives of this trend take such pride, constitute only a mounting for introspection, an objective-scientific frame for a subjective-internal picture—and no more.

The question inevitably arises as to whether the "inner experience" of the subject does not in fact compromise the *integrity and consistency* of the experimenter's external apprehension. Does not this *inner point of view* (the subject after all reports his experience from an inner point of view) bring to bear *something incompatible with the data of external apprehension*, something fundamentally insusceptible to objective analysis and measurement?

That is precisely what the representatives of objective psychology maintain. They argue that it is impossible to construct an exact and objective science if the method of self-observation, which the subjectivists accept, is used. It is essential, they insist, that the point of view of external, objective apprehension be adhered to consistently and throughout if a scientific psychology is to be constructed. Meanwhile, the introduction of introspective data destroys the integrity and the consistency of external apprehension. Everything in life, everything in practice that can have meaning must, after all, be presented as an external, material quantity, must be expressed in some purely material index of change.[7]

Such purely material quantities are the various *reactions of a living organism to stimuli*. Taken together, these reactions make up what we call the behavior of a human being or an animal.

This behavior of a living organism is wholly accessible to *external, objective apprehension*; everything of which it is comprised can be calculated, measured and brought into the necessary *cause-and-effect relation* with external stimuli and the conditions of the surrounding material environment. *Only this materially expressed behavior of the human and the animal can constitute the object of study in a psychology that wants to be exact and objective.* Such is the position of the objectivists.

A psychological experiment—for, of course, the objectivists, too, must use experiments—must be localized throughout its entire extent in the external world, and all its factors must be accessible to the experimenter. It is totally inadmissible for an objectivist to deal with the data of both internal and external observation *on one and the same plane* of material apprehension, as a subjectivist does. Inevitably *double formations* will arise, confusion set in, and the unity and integrity of external, material apprehension be undermined. The subject's "inner experience" must also be translated somehow into the language of external apprehension, and only in that shape can it be taken into account by the experimenter.

For *external* apprehension, what corresponds to inner experience are the subject's *words*, the words with the help of which he reports that experience.

---

[7] In the interests of accuracy, it should be noted that the behaviorists, while rejecting introspection as a scientific method of investigation, do, nevertheless, consider that, owing to the present state of psychology as a science, introspection should be used in certain cases where it is the only immediately available means of observation. See Watson, *Psychology.* [*Editor's note*]

This kind of expression of experience has been given the name *verbal reaction* (or "verbal account," in the terminology of the behaviorists).

Verbal reaction is a phenomenon of the highest complexity. It consists of the following components:

1. *The physical sound of articulated words;*

2. *Physiological processes in the nervous system and in the organs of speech and perception;*

3. *A special set of features and processes that correspond to the "meaning" of a verbal statement and the "understanding" of that meaning by another person or persons.* This set is not subject to purely physiological interpretation, since the phenomena entailed *transcend the limits of a single, isolated physiological organism and always involve the interaction of organisms.* This third component of verbal reaction is, thus, *sociological* in character. The formation of verbal meanings requires the establishment of connections among visual, motor, and auditory reactions over the course of long and organized social intercourse between individuals. However, this set, too, is completely objective inasmuch as all the ways and means that serve the formation of verbal connections fall within external apprehension and are on principle accessible to objective methods of study, even if these methods are not purely physiological ones.

The complex apparatus of verbal reactions functions in all its fundamental aspects also when the subject says nothing about his experiences but only undergoes them "in himself," since, if he is conscious of them, a process of *inner* ("covert") speech occurs (we do, after all, think and feel and desire with the help of words; without inner speech we would not become conscious of anything in ourselves). This process of inner speech is just as material as is outward speech.[8]

And so, if in a psychological experiment we replace the subject's "inner experience" with its *verbal equivalent* (inner and outward speech or only inner speech), we still can maintain the integrity and consistency of external, material apprehension. That is how a psychological experiment is viewed by the objectivists.

We have now identified the two trends in modern psychology.

Which of them is in closer correspondence to the basic principles of dialectical materialism? Of course it is the second, the objective trend in psychology. It alone answers the requirements of *materialistic monism.*

Marxism is far from denying the reality of the *subjective-psychical.* Such a thing does exist, to be sure, but under no circumstances can it be divorced from

[8] On verbal reactions, see *ibid.*, Chapter 9, and the article by L. S. Vygotskij, "Soznanie kak problema psixologii povedenija" [Consciousness as a Problem in the Pschology of Behavior], in *Psixologija i Marksizm*, ed. Kornilov (Leningrad, GIZ, 1925).

the *material basis* of the organism's behavior. *The psychical is only one of the properties of organized matter* and, therefore, it does not allow of being placed in opposition to the material, on the order of a special hermeneutical principle. On the contrary, what is essential is to make clear, operating entirely on the grounds of external, material apprehension, under what kind of organization and at what degree of complexity of matter this new quality—the psychical—comes about, it being a property of the very matter itself. Internal, subjective apprehension cannot possibly make the slightest contribution toward that end. In this respect objective psychology is entirely correct.

However, dialectical materialism places still another, very important demand on psychology, a demand by no means always taken into account and implemented by the objectivists: *human* psychology must be *socialized*.

And indeed, is it possible to understand human behavior without bringing to bear an *objective-sociological* point of view? All the fundamental and essential acts in human life are brought about by social stimuli in conditions of a social environment. If we know only the physical component of the stimulus and the abstracted physiological component of the reaction, we still understand exceedingly little about a human act.

To cite an example: The verbal reactions that play so great a role in human behavior (since every single conscious human act is accompanied by inner speech) are not amenable, as we have seen, to purely physiological methods of study; they constitute a specifically *social* manifestation of the human organism.

The formation of verbal reactions is possible only in conditions of a social environment. The complex apparatus of verbal connections is worked out and put into practice in a process of long, organized, and multilateral contact among organisms. Psychology cannot, of course, dispense with objective, sociological methods.

In sum, then, psychology must implement *objective methods* and study the *materially expressed behavior of human beings* in conditions of the natural and the *social* environment. Such are the requirements that Marxism makes incumbent upon psychology.

What position does psychoanalysis occupy in the controversy of modern psychological trends?

Freudians, as indeed Freud himself, look upon the Freudian doctrine as the first and only attempt at constructing a truly objective, naturalistic psychology. Russian psychological and philosophical literature, as we pointed out earlier, contains a number of works which try to prove that these claims of psychoanalysis are correct and that in its fundamentals (with, of course, various changes and additions in matters of detail) psychoanalysis best answers the Marxist requirements for a science of psychology.[9] Other representatives of objective psychology

---

[9] A. B. Zalkind, *Frejdizm i marksizm (Očerki kul'tury revoljucionnogo vremeni)* [Freudianism and Marxism (Essays in the Culture of Revolutionary Times)]; an article under

and of Marxism take a different view of psychoanalysis, considering it totally unacceptable from an objective-materialistic point of view.[10]

This issue is an interesting and very important one.

Objective psychology is a young discipline; it is still only beginning to take shape. The way it can best clarify its *point of view* and *methods* is by intelligently criticizing and combating other trends (not to speak, of course, of its direct task of working with the material of behavior). Such efforts will help it become *methodologically* sounder and better able to formulate its position precisely.

Objective psychology is threatened by a certain, quite serious danger—the danger of falling into *naive, mechanistic materialism*. This danger is comparatively mild in those fields of the natural sciences that deal with inorganic nature, but it becomes considerably more serious in biology. *In psychology, a simplistic, mechanistic materialism could well play a disastrous role.* Just such a turn in the direction of primitive materialism and its concomitant *simplification* of the tasks of objective psychology is detectable among the American behaviorists and the Russian reflexologists.

It is precisely when objective psychology confronts the necessity of taking a clearcut critical position with regard to all those complex and extremely important issues raised by psychoanalysis that the insufficiency and crudity of simplistic physiological approaches to human behavior are vividly exposed. At the same time, the necessity of applying a *dialectical and sociological point of view* in psychology becomes manifestly obvious.

The fact is that *critical analysis of Freud's psychological theory will bring us directly in contact with precisely the issue that is of utmost importance and difficulty in human psychology—the issue of verbal reactions and their meaning in human behavior as a whole.*

We shall see that all of the mental phenomena and conflicts that psychoanalysis acquaints us with may be *regarded as complex interrelations and conflicts between the verbal and the nonverbal reactions of humans*.

We shall see that within the verbal domain of human behavior very substantial *conflicts* take place between *inner speech* and *outward speech* and between

the same title appeared in *Krasnaja Nov'* 4 (1924); *Žizn' organizma i vnušenie* [The Life of the Organism and the Method of Suggestion] (GIZ, 1927), Chapters 7, 8, and 16. B. Bykovskij, "O metodologičeskix osnovanijax psixoanalitičeskogo učenija Frejda" [On the Methodological Bases of Freud's Psychoanalytical Doctrine], *Pod znamenem Marksizma* 12 (1923). B. D. Fridman, "Osnovnye psixologičeskie vozzrenija Frejda i teorija istoričeskogc materializma" [Freud's Basic Psychological Views and the Theory of Historical Materialism], in Kornilov, *Psixologija i Marksizm*. A. R. Luria, "Psixoanaliz kak sistema monističeskoj psixologii" [Psychoanalysis as a System of Monistic Psychology], in *ibid*.
[10] See V. Jurinec, "Frejdizm i marksizm" [Freudianism and Marxism], *Pod znamenem marksizma* 8-9 (1924), and our article, "Po tu storonu social'nogo" [Beyond the Social], *Zvezda* 5 (1925).

different levels of inner speech. We shall see that the formation of verbal connections (the establishment of connections among visual, motor, and other kinds of reactions over the course of interindividual communication, upon which the formation of verbal reactions depends) proceeds with special difficulty and delay in certain areas of life (for example, the sexual). In the language of Freud, all of this is spoken of as conflicts between the conscious and the unconscious.[11]

Freud's strength lies in his having brought these issues pointedly to the fore and in having gathered the material for their investigation. His weakness lies in his having failed to understand the sociological essence of all these phenomena and in having attempted, instead, to force them into the narrow confines of the individual organism and its psyche. *Processes that are in fact social are treated by Freud from the point of view of individual psychology.*

With this disregard of sociology is coupled another basic deficiency in Freud—the *subjectivity of his method* (granted, a subjectivity somewhat disguised, for which reason it has been a debatable feature). Freud does not consistently and thoroughly maintain the point of view of external, objective apprehension and does attempt to shed light on conflicts in human behavior from within, that is, from the introspective point of view (but again, we repeat, in somewhat disguised form). Thus, his interpretation of the facts and phenomena under his scrutiny is, as we hope to convince the reader, fundamentally unacceptable.

Another problem that arises no less pointedly from a critical evaluation of Freudianism is closely connected with the first problem of verbal reactions. This has to do with the "content of the psyche"—a content consisting of thoughts, desires, dreams, and so forth.[12] This "content of the psyche" is *ideological through and through; from the vaguest of thoughts and dimmest and most uncertain of desires all the way to philosophical systems and complex political institutions, we have one continuous series of ideological and, hence also, sociological phenomena.* Not a single member of this series from one end to the other is the product solely of individual organic creativity. The vaguest of thoughts—even one that remains unarticulated—and a whole complex philosophical movement both equally presuppose organized interindividual communication (allowing, of course, for various kinds and degrees of organization in it). Freud, meanwhile, would have the entire ideological series from one end to the other develop out of the simplest elements of the individual psyche in what amounts to a socially vacuous atmosphere.

[11] It should be pointed out that Freud, too, knows a definition of the unconscious as a "non-verbal" entity. Something more on this point will be mentioned later.

[12] Strictly speaking, this is the other side of the same problem since the content of the psyche becomes known to us with the aid of inner speech.

We have here done no more than make preliminary mention of the two cardinal problems in psychology. But we consider it vital that the reader keep these problems constantly in view when following the exposition of psychoanalysis to come.

Now, to conclude this chapter, we must touch upon one other question that we mentioned in passing at the beginning of the chapter.

From what we have already said by way of preliminary orientation, the reader can clearly see that the psychological, that is, the technical-scientific, side of Freudianism is by no means neutral with respect to its general ideological and class position—a position so vividly expressed in its basic philosophical motif.

Not everybody agrees on this point. Many people believe that the *special scientific disciplines* can and should treat their topics in a way completely independent of general world outlook. In the current debate over the object and the methods of study in psychology, certain professionals have advanced the notion of the *higher-level neutrality of the special scientific disciplines, and of psychology among them, in all matters of world outlook and social orientation.*

We believe that that neutrality is a complete fiction. For *sociological* as well as *logical* reasons, such neutrality is impossible.

In point of fact, only if we have not thought through a scientific theory can we fail to notice *its essential connection with basic issues of world outlook*; once we subject it to thoroughgoing scrutiny, any such theory will inevitably reveal a general philosophical orientation.

Thus, subjective psychology in all its various tendencies, provided it follows a consistent development methodologically, inevitably leads to dualism, that is, to the splitting up of being into two incompatible aspects—the material and the mental—or leads to a purely *idealistic* monism. That most seemingly innocent scrap of the "experienced from within," which, as we have seen, undermines the integrity of the objective-material conduct of an experiment in the laboratory, can also serve perfectly well as an Archimedean fulcrum for the break-up of the objective-materialistic picture of the world as a whole.

Scientific neutrality is also impossible in a sociological sense. After all, there is no reason to trust the *subjective sincerity* of human views even at their most earnest. Class interest and presumption constitute an *objective* sociological category of which the *individual* psyche is by no means always aware. But it is precisely *class* interest wherein the power of any theory, of any thought, resides. For indeed, if a thought is powerful, convincing, significant, then obviously it has succeeded in contacting *essential* aspects in the life of the social group in question, succeeded in making a connection between itself and the basic position of that group in the *class struggle*, despite the fact that the creator of that thought might himself be wholly unaware of having done so. The degree of the efficacy and significance of thoughts is directly proportional to their *class-groundedness*, their *ability to be fructified by the socioeconomic being of the*

group in question. Let us recall that verbal reactions are a purely social formation. All the enduring, *constant* factors in these reactions are factors precisely of
class-consciousness and *not of personal* self-conscious.

Human thought never reflects merely the object under scrutiny. It also
reflects, along with that object, the being of the scrutinizing subject, his concrete
social existence. Thought is a two-sided mirror, and both its sides can and should
be clear and unobscured. Exactly what we shall try to do is to understand both
sides of Freudian thought.

We have now sufficiently oriented ourselves with respect to basic trends, both
in modern philosophy and in modern psychology, and we have acquainted
ourselves with the Marxist criteria. We are now equipped with the thread to
mark our passage and can plunge ahead into the labyrinth of psychoanalysis.

PART II

AN EXPOSITION
OF FREUDIANISM

CHAPTER 3

The Unconscious and the
Dynamics of the Psyche

The conscious and the unconscious. Three periods in the development of Freudianism. The first concept of the unconscious. The method of catharsis. Special features of the first period. The theory of repression.

The human psyche, according to Freud, is divided into three regions: the *conscious*, the *unconscious*, and the *preconscious*. These three regions, or "systems," of the psyche are in a state of incessant interaction, the first two being, additionally, in a state of incessant conflict between themselves. This interaction and this conflict are what the psychical life of human beings amounts to. Each mental act, each manifestation of human behavior, is to be regarded as a *result of the competition and conflict between the conscious and the unconscious—an index of the correlation, reached at a given moment of life, in the power struggle between these two ever-opposing sides.*

Were we to listen only to what the conscious tells us about our mental life, we should never understand that life. The conscious, incessantly struggling with the unconscious, always operates tendentiously. It presents us deliberate falsifications both about itself and about our psychical life in its totality. Yet, psychology had always based its postulates on the evidence of the conscious, and, what is more, the majority of psychologists had simply identified the conscious with the psychical altogether. The few exceptions, such as Lipps and Charcot and his school, who did take the unconscious into account, utterly underestimated its psychical role. They imagined the unconscious to be a kind of absolutely predetermined and stable addendum to mental life. The perpetual dynamics of its conflict with the conscious remained beyond their ken. As a result of this identification of the psychical with consciousness, the older psychology had, in Freud's view, painted a wholly false picture of our psyche, inasmuch as the *primary mass* of the psychical and its *primary centers of power* do in fact fall within the region of the unconscious.

The excitement of Freudianism was the excitement of discovering a whole new world, an unknown continent on the other side of culture and history, but a world that was, at the same time, *extraordinarily close to us,* ready at any moment to erupt through the crust of our consciousness and find reflection in our utterances, our slips of the tongue, our gestures, our behavior.

The proximity of the unconscious and the ease with which it infiltrates the most prosaic matters in life, reaching into the very sum and substance of everyday existence, constitute basic features whereby Freud's theory is distinguished from the doctrines of such high-style "philosophies of the unconscious" as those of Schopenhauer and, especially, Hartmann.

The concept of the unconscious did not acquire instant shape and definition in Freud's mind; it underwent substantial changes as time went on. We see three periods in the history of its development.

In the first period (what might be called the Freud-Breuer period), the Freudian concept of the unconscious was close to the teachings of the eminent French psychiatrists and psychologists Charcot, Lièbault, Bernheim, and Janet. In fact there was direct lineal descent, inasmuch as Freud had studied under Charcot and Bernheim.

The approximate time boundaries of the first period are the years 1890-1897. The basic (and only) book representing that period was Freud and Breuer's *Studien über Hysterie,* which came out in 1895.

During the second, the longest, and the most important period in the development of psychoanalysis, all the basic and characteristic features of the Freudian doctrine on the unconscious took definitive shape. That doctrine became wholly original. All issues during this period were dealt with exclusively *on the level of theoretical and applied psychology.* Freud still avoided making broad philosophical generalizations and dealing with questions of Weltanschauung. The whole idea of the unconscious bore an emphatically *positivistic character.*[1] The style of Freud's works during this period was dry and business-like. The approximate chronological boundaries of this second period are the

---

[1] Even at the present time (1927) Freud still insists upon the strictly empirical nature of his doctrine. According to him, psychoanalysis "is not a philosophical system; it is not derived from a set of rigorously defined premises; it does not aim at encompassing the totality of the world with the aid of those premises; and it does not represent a perfected body of thought that precludes new findings and better reflection." On the contrary, psychoanalysis, he claims, "is based on the facts provided by the field of inquiry, aims at solving the immediate problems that arise from observation . . . , and is always unfinished, always prepared to enter corrections into its theories." *Handwörterbuch der Sexualwissenschaft,* p. 616. [*Editor's note*]

years 1897-1914. During this period all of Freud's basic psychoanalytical works were issued.[2]

In the third, and current, period, the conception of the unconscious has undergone substantial changes (particularly in the works of Freud's students and followers) and has begun to approach the metaphysical doctrines of Schopenhauer and Hartmann. *General issues of Weltanschauung now begin to take precedence over particular, specialized problems.* The unconscious becomes the embodiment of all that belongs both to the lowest and to the highest levels in man (mainly for representatives of the Swiss school of Freudianism). The doctrine on the superego (*Ich-Ideal*) makes its appearance.

How are these changes in the very spirit of the Freudian doctrine to be explained?

The explanation lies partly in the direct influence of Schopenhauer and Hartmann (Nietzsche, as well) whom Freud had begun to study diligently by this time. Previously, throughout the first period and most of the second, Freud, as a consistent positivist, had ignored philosophy.[3] These changes are also partly an expression of the powerful influence of certain of Freud's newer followers who have always been attuned to philosophical and humanistic considerations and who brought this new note into the discussion of psychoanalytical questions (especially Otto Rank and Ferenczi). However, the main role in these changes was most likely played by the reverse influence on Freud of the public whose enthusiasm he had so aroused. Freud, by the time the third period begins, had become an acknowledged "celebrity" for wide circles of the intelligentsia. And these circles had already endeavored to ferret out precisely philosophical, ideological themes, even from Freud's earliest works. They expected and demanded of psychoanalysis a "revelation" in the domain of Weltanschauung. And so Freud bit by bit succumbed and began to cater to those demands and expectations. What took place is a common enough phenomenon. Success and recognition compromised and somewhat perverted a doctrine that had originally taken shape and had flourished in an atmosphere of hostility and rejection.

The approximate boundary between this third and last period and the second one runs somewhere around 1914-1915.[4] The basic writings of this period are Freud's two most recent books: *Jenseits des Lustprincips* and *Das Ich und das Es.* However, the most striking expression was given this period not in the

---

[2] *Traumdeutung* (1900); *Psychopathologie des Alltagsleben* (1901); *Der Witz* (1905); *Drei Abhandlungen zur Sexualtheorie* (1905). Finally, three basic volumes of the *Kleine Schriften zur Neurosenlehre* and a host of other, lesser works.

[3] See note 1, above. [Editor's note]

[4] The first characteristic notes of the last stage of Freudianism began to be struck in such works as *Einführung des Narzissmus* and *Trauer und Melancholie.*

writings of Freud himself but of his favorite student, Otto Rank, whose sensation-producing volume, *The Trauma of Birth,*[5] appeared three years ago (1924). Rank's book is the most characteristic expression of the new spirit that has come to prevail in psychoanalysis today. It is a philosophical tome from start to finish. It is written in the tone and style of a sage "making great and awesome pronouncements." In places it suggests a low-grade parody on the Nietzsche of the Schopenhauer phase.[6] Rank's conclusions are astonishingly extreme. In the dry and sober atmosphere of the second, classical, period of psychoanalysis such a book would have been a total impossibility.

We have now outlined the three periods in the development of psychoanalysis. The differences and peculiarities of each must always be kept in mind; they cannot be ignored for the sake of constructing a logical unity. Throughout the 33 years of its historical existence psychoanalysis has changed in many and important ways. It no longer is what it was on the eve of World War I.

What is the "unconscious"? How was it first formulated in the earliest period of the development of psychoanalysis?

Back in 1889, while he was in Nancy, Freud, then a young Viennese doctor, was extremely impressed with an experiment conducted by the famous expert in hypnosis, Bernheim. A woman patient was hypnotized and instructed to walk to the corner of the room and open an umbrella that was standing there, and to perform these actions at a certain designated time after awakening. Upon awakening and after the designated time period had elapsed, the woman carried out precisely what she had been instructed to do: She walked over to the corner of the room and opened the umbrella in the room. Questioned as to what had made her do that, she responded that she wished to ascertain whether the umbrella was hers. This motive did not in the least correspond to the real reason for the act and obviously had been thought up post factum, but it was perfectly satisfactory for the patient's consciousness. She was sincerely convinced that she had opened the umbrella of her own volition with the aim of determining whether it belonged to her. Later, Bernheim, by persistently questioning the patient and leading her thoughts, finally made her remember the real reason for her act, that is, the instructions she had received under hypnosis.[7]

From this experiment Freud drew three general conclusions that laid the foundations for his earliest conception of the unconscious:

1. *For all its subjective sincerity, the conscious does not always supply a motivation corresponding to the real reasons for an act.*

[5] Trauma der Geburt (1924).

[6] Nietzsche's *Birth of Tragedy*, from which Rank took the epigraph for his book.

[7] See Freud, "Zur Geschichte der psychoanalytischen Bewegung," in *Kleine Schriften zur Neurosenlehre*, Part 4.

2. *An act can sometimes be determined by forces that operate in the psyche but do not reach the conscious.*
3. *With the help of certain techniques, these psychical forces can be brought to consciousness.*

On the basis of these propositions, which were verified by his own psychiatric practice, Freud, in collaboration with his older colleague, Breuer, worked out what was called the "cathartic method of treating hysteria."[8]

The gist of this method consists in the following. At the basis of hysteria and other *psychogenic* nervous disorders lie psychical complexes submerged below the conscious of the patient. Involved here are various possible mental disturbances, feelings, or desires that the patient had once experienced but then had *deliberately forgotten* because his conscious, for one reason or another, was afraid or ashamed of remembering them. Without surfacing in the conscious, these forgotten experiences cannot be "lived out" and "worked through" (or "discharged") in the normal way. Just such experiences cause the pathological symptoms of hysteria. The doctor's efforts are supposed to remove the *amnesia* in which these experiences are held, to bring them to the patient's conscious, to integrate them with that conscious and thereby make it possible for these experiences to be lived out and discharged without hindrance. By means of such a process of "living out" the pathological symptoms of hysteria are done away with.

To take a hypothetical example: A young lady feels toward a closely related person a kind of attraction, which from her own point of view seems so inadmissible, so bizarre, so unnatural that she cannot acknowledge that feeling even to herself. Therefore, she is in no position to subject that feeling to responsible and conscious discussion even in private with herself. Such an experience, which she herself cannot acknowledge, will assume in the young lady's psyche a completely *isolated status*; it will not be able to enter into any connection with other experiences, thoughts, considerations. Fear, shame, and indignation will drive that experience into severe mental exile. In its isolated state, this experience cannot find a way out of exile, since the normal outlet would be some kind of action, some form of behavior, or, at least, the discourse and reasoned arguments of consciousness. But all such outlets are closed. The isolated experience, hemmed in on all sides (or "bracketed"—*eingeklemmte*, as Freud puts it), begins to seek an outlet along abnormal routes where it might remain unrecognized—for example, in the paralysis of some perfectly healthy limb, in causeless outbreaks of terror, in some kind of nonsensical activity, and so on. Thereby the symptoms of hysteria take shape. The doctor's task in the

---

[8] For all that follows here, see Freud and Breuer, *Studien über Hysterie*, 1st edition [1895]; 4th edition [1922] or the article by Freud in *Handwörterbuch*, p. 160.

given instance amounts primarily to discovering from the patient the reason for her illness, a reason she has forgotten and cannot acknowledge, and forcing her to call it to mind. (For this purpose, Freud and Breuer used either full or partial hypnosis.) Once having discovered the reason for the illness, the doctor must force the patient, while helping her overcome her fear and shame, to stop "camouflaging" it in hysterical symptoms and to engage it into the "normal workings" of her consciousness. In doing this, the doctor makes it possible for the experience to discharge normally, either by way of conscious struggle with it or, at times, by way of expedient concessions to it. Perhaps our young lady patient will have to contend with severe adversity or embarrassments in her life, but she will no longer have to contend with illness. The hysterical symptoms will become superfluous and gradually will cease.

To this liberation from a fearful and shameful experience via the "living out" of the experience Freud applied the Aristotelean term "catharsis" (in Aristotle's theory of poetics, tragedy purges the spectators' souls of the effects of pity and terror by making the spectators experience these feelings in diluted form). Hence the name given by Freud and Breuer to their method—the "cathartic method."

The "unconscious," as Freud understood it in the first period of the development of his doctrine, was comprised of just such forgotten experiences that caused symptoms of hysteria. This version of the unconscious defined it as a sort of *foreign body* that penetrated into the psyche. Such a foreign body did not have firm associational bonds with other factors in the psyche and thus disrupted its integrity. A close counterpart in normal life was the state of daydreaming, since it, too, was freer of the tight associational bonds that infiltrate our consciousness than were real-life experiences. Another close counterpart was the hypnotic state, for which reason Freud and Breur called the unconscious the "hypnoid."

Such was Freud's earliest conception of the unconscious.

Let us now note and underscore two special features of it. First, Freud did not provide us any physiological theory of the unconscious, nor did he make any attempt to do so—in contrast to Breuer, who did propose physiological substantiation for his method. Freud, on the contrary, *turned his back on physiology from the very start*. Second, the products of the unconscious were obtainable only *in translation into the language of consciousness*. There was no direct access possible to the unconscious other than the conscious of the patient himself.

We must once again point out to the reader the enormous importance that the cathartic method attached to *verbal reactions*. Freud himself made explicit reference to this feature of his theory. He compared his method of treating hysteria with the confession in the Catholic church. At confession, a believer really does obtain relief and purification thanks to his telling another person, in this case, the priest, about thoughts and acts that he himself considers sinful and that he could not, under other circumstances, have told to anyone. In this way he gives *verbal expression* and *verbal outlet* to what was bottled up inside and isolated in his psyche and had been oppressing it. Therein lies the cleansing power of speech.[9]

Now we must proceed to the further development of the concept of the unconscious that took place in the second, classical, period of psychoanalysis. Here, the concept of the unconscious became enriched with a host of new and most vital factors.

During the first period, the unconscious had been conceived of, to a certain degree, as an *incidental phenomenon* in the human psyche—a sort of pathological addendum, a foreign body that had penetrated the psyche of an hysterically inclined person under the influence of chance circumstances in that person's life. The normal psychical apparatus was conceived of, during the same period, as something entirely static and steadfast. *The conflict of psychical forces was not at all regarded as a constant and regular form of mental life* but, rather, as an *exceptional and abnormal occurrence in it*. Moreover, the content of the unconscious remained entirely unelucidated and also seems to have been regarded as fortuitous. Depending on a person's individual characteristics and on chance circumstances in his life, some painful or shameful experience is isolated and forgotten and becomes unconscious. No *typological generalizations* about such experiences were made by Freud. The exceptional significance of the sexual factor had not yet been advanced. Such was the state of affairs during the first period.

Now, in the second period, the unconscious becomes an essential and extremely vital component of the psychical apparatus of every single human being. The very psychical apparatus itself becomes *dynamic*, that is, is set into perpetual motion. The conflict between the conscious and the unconscious is declared a constant and regular form of psychical life. The unconscious, moreover, becomes a productive source of psychical forces and energies for all domains of cultural creativity, especially for art. At the same time, the unconscious can become the source of all nervous disorders whenever its conflict with the conscious goes awry.

According to these new views of Freud's, the process of formation of the unconscious is a perfectly regular phenomenon and takes place throughout a person's life, starting from the very moment of birth. The process itself is termed "repression" (*Verdrängung*). Repression is one of the most important concepts of the entire psychoanalytical doctrine. Furthermore, during this same period,

---

[9] It should be noted that Freud, in this same period, had stopped using hypnosis for cathartic purposes in his own psychiatric practice and had replaced it with the method of free association. By persistent questioning and long observation the doctor, having first prepared the patient, explores for those "shameful and fearful" experiences that have been driven deep into the unconscious and, finding them, brings them to the patient's consciousness where they are able to discharge naturally. [*Editor's note*]

the content of the unconscious is typologized. No longer does that content consist of incidental and arbitrary experiences but, rather, of certain bound sets of experiences (complexes) that are typical for and fundamentally *common* to all human beings and bear a specific—primarily sexual—character. These *complexes* are repressed into the unconscious *at certain strictly defined periods* that occur and recur throughout the history of the life of every human being.

In the present chapter, we shall familiarize ourselves with the basic psychical "mechanism" of repression and the concept of "censorship" closely associated with it. The content of the unconscious we shall leave for the following chapter.

What is repression?

In the early stages of the development of the human personality, our psyche knows no distinction between the possible and the impossible, the beneficial and the harmful, the permissible and the forbidden. It is governed by one principle alone—the "pleasure principle" (*Lustprincip*).[10] At the dawn of the development of the human soul, free and unhampered play is enjoyed by notions, feelings, desires that at later stages of development would horrify the conscious. In the child's soul "all is permitted." There are for it no immoral feelings and desires, and, not knowing fear or shame, it makes broad use of this privilege, accumulating a huge store of the most depraved images, feelings, and desires— "depraved" from the point of view of later stages of development, needless to say. To this unbounded domination of the pleasure principle is joined, at the very earliest stage of development, the ability to achieve *hallucinatory satisfaction of desires,* seeing that an infant cannot yet tell the difference between what is real and what is not. For an infant, a mental representation is already the real thing. Hallucinatory satisfaction of desires (wish fulfillment) is retained by human beings throughout life in dreams.[11]

At later stages of development, the pleasure principle relinquishes its exclusive hold over the psyche; along with it—often in spite of it—a new principle of psychical life begins to operate. This is the "reality principle." All psychical events must now pass a *double examination* from the viewpoints of both these principles. Indeed, a desire may turn out to be unsatisfiable and therefore a cause of suffering or a desire, once satisfied, may bring on disagreeable consequences. Such desires must be suppressed. A mental presentation may be closely linked by association with feelings of fear or remembrances of pain. Such images must be kept from emerging in the psyche.

Thus, a process of psychical selection comes about, and only mental formations that pass the twofold test from the viewpoints of both principles are legitimized and enfranchised, so to speak, and either enter into the higher system

[10] Freud, "Über zwei Princip des psychologischen Geschehens," in *Kleine Schriften zur Neurosenlehre*, Part 3, p. 271.

[11] See *Traumdeutung*.

of the psyche—the *conscious*—or acquire the possibility of doing so, thus becoming the *preconscious*. Meanwhile, experiences that do not pass the test become illegitimate and are repressed into the system of the *unconscious*.

This repression is accomplished *automatically, without any participation of the conscious*, and operates this way throughout a person's entire life. The conscious comes into being fully-fledged and purified; items that have been repressed do not register in the conscious and it may totally lack the slightest inkling of their presence or makeup. What takes charge of repression is another, special psychical force that Freud picturesquely termed the "censorship." The censorship occupies a position on the border between the systems of the unconscious and the conscious. Everything that has come into the conscious, or has the possibility of doing so, has undergone a rigorous process of censorship.[12]

The entire mass of "uncensored" presentations, feeling and desires repressed into the unconscious *never expires* and never loses its power. Indeed, a feeling or desire can only be "lived out" and gotten rid of through the conscious and through the actions and behavior it controls—above all, human speech. The unconscious is nonverbal, it abhors words. We cannot acknowledge our unconscious desires even to ourselves in inner speech. Consequently, these desires have no way out; they cannot be worked through, and, therefore, they go on living in our psyche with their full power and vitality unimpaired.[13]

Such is the way the process of repression works.

We can now define the unconscious, in terms of the *psychical dynamics* of its formation, as *the repressed*. What character the repressed bears or, in other words, what its content is, we shall elucidate in the next chapter.

---

[12] On this point, in addition to *Traumdeutung*, see *Das Ich und das Es*, Chapters 1 and 2.

[13] *Jenseits des Lustprincips*, pp. 35-36; and *Kleine Schriften zur Neurosenlehre*, Part 4: "Das Unbewusste."

CHAPTER 4

The Content of
the Unconscious

The theory of instincts. The sexual life of the child. The Oedipus Complex. The content of the unconscious in the second period of Freudianism. The theory of instincts in the third period (Eros and Death). The Super-ego.

We are now acquainted with the operation of repression. The next question is: Where does the material for repression come from?

Exactly what kind of feelings, desires, mental presentations are repressed into the unconscious?

In order to understand what is at issue here—that is, in order to be able to deal with the content of the unconscious—we must familiarize ourselves with Freud's *theory of instincts* (*Triebe*).[1]

Psychical activity is set in motion by *external and internal stimuli* on the organism. Internal stimuli have a somatic source, that is, they originate within our organism. The psychical counterparts of these internal, somatic *stimuli* are what Freud calls the *instincts*.

Freud divides all instincts into two sets according to their aims and somatic source:

1. *Sexual instincts, the aim of which is the continuation of the species even at the cost of the individual's life;*

2. *Personal or ego instincts (Ich-triebe), the aim of which is individual self-preservation.*

Neither of these two sets is reducible to the other, and they often enter into mutual conflicts of various kinds.

[1] "Triebe und Triebschicksale," in *Kleine Schriften zur Neurosenlehre; Das Ich und das Es,* Chapter 4.

Here we shall be concerned only with the sexual instincts, since they provide the main bulk of the material for the unconscious. This set of instincts has been thoroughly investigated by Freud.[2] A number of people maintain that the chief merits of Freudianism lie precisely in the domain of sexual theory.

We mentioned in the preceding chapter that the child, at the earliest stages of his psychical life, amasses an enormous store of feelings and desires that are depraved and immoral from the point of view of the conscious. To the reader unacquainted with Freud that assertion no doubt seemed very odd and possibly even caused some perplexity. Indeed, where in the world does a child get immoral, depraved desires? A child, after all, is the very symbol of innocence and purity!

The sexual instinct or, to use another Freudian term, the *libido* is inherent in the child from the very start of his life; it originates with the birth of his body and carries on a permanent existence in his organism and psyche, an existence that may from time to time lose force but never is altogether extinguished. Sexual maturity is only one stage—granted, a stage of great importance—in the development of sexuality but by no means its point of origin.

During those early stages of development wherein the pleasure principle, with its "all is permitted," reigns supreme, the sexual instinct has the following distinguishing characteristics:

1. The genitals have not yet become the somatic organizing center of the sexual instinct; they are only one set of so-called "erogenous zones" and are in equal competition with other zones of the body such as, for example, the oral cavity (in the act of sucking), the anus or anal zone (in the act of defecating), the skin, the thumb, the big toe, and the like. It could be claimed that the sexual instinct, or libido, of the child, before it can focus and concentrate in the as yet immature sexual organs, is diffused throughout the child's body, so that any part of that body whatsoever is capable of becoming a somatic source of sexual arousal. In view of the fact that at this stage the sexual organs, the genitals, have not yet become the body's center for the sexual instinct, Freud has named it the "pregenital stage." It should be noted that a certain degree of sexual arousal still remains possible for the erogenous zones (especially the mouth and the anus) throughout the entire remainder of a person's life.[3]

[2] For the exposition that follows, see Freud, *Drei Abhandlungen zur Sexualtheorie* (1905).

[3] The development of the sexual instinct in the child passes through the following stages, according to Freud. The first pregenital stage is the oral stage, wherein the mouth plays the principal role, in compliance with the child's most essential interests; the next stage is the anal stage; finally, the last stage is reached when the genital zone occupies the prime position. In Freud's view, the child passes through all these stages quite rapidly—within the course of four to five years after birth. [*Editor's note*]

2. A child's sexual instinct is *not yet autonomous or differentiated*; it joins in closely with other needs of the organism and the processes of their satisfaction—the processes of eating, suckling, urination, defecation, and others, thereby imbuing all these other processes with a *sexual coloration*.

3. A child's sexual instinct in its first, "oral" stage can be satisfied *by his own body* without need for an *object* (another person). *The child*, therefore, *is autoerotic*.

4. Since the primacy of the genitals, their predominance in sexual life, has not yet been established, the sexual discrimination of the child is in an ambiguous state. It can be claimed, then, that in its earliest development the sexual instinct is *bisexual*.

5. As a result of all these features in the early development of the sexual instinct, the child is a *polymorph pervers*: He is susceptible to masochism, sadism, homosexuality, and other perversions. This is a natural consequence of the fact that his libido is diffused throughout his body and can join with any process or organic sensation, deriving sexual pleasure from it. What the child is least able to understand is precisely the normal sex act. As regards the sexual perversions of adults, Freud considers them a phenomenon of *retarded normal development*, a regression to earlier stages of infantile sexuality.

Such are, according to Freud, the main features of infantile eroticism.

We can now more clearly appreciate the huge store of sexual desires, and the images and feelings connected with them, that can come about in a child's psyche, grounded in the infantile libido, and must afterward be mercilessly repressed into the unconscious.

We may say that the entire early period in the history of our psyche takes place outside the boundaries of consciousness—indeed, rarely do people recall what happened to them before the age of four. Nevertheless, the events of that period do not lose their power but remain alive in our unconscious; this is "past history" that has not died but perseveres in the present inasmuch as it has not been "lived out."

The most important event in the repressed history of infantile sexual life is the child's *sexual attraction to his mother* and, coupled with it, *hatred for his father*—the so-called *Oedipus complex*.[4] The doctrine on this complex and its role in human life is one of the most crucial points in Freudianism. The gist of it amounts to the following. The first object of a human being's sexual instinct—*sexual* in the sense of infantile eroticism as characterized above—is his *mother*. A child's relationship with his mother is acutely *sexualized* from the very start. According to Otto Rank, the authoritative disciple of Freud whom we have

---

[4] On this, see Freud, *Traumdeutung*; Jung, *Die Bedeutung des Vaters für das Schiksal des Einzelnen*; and O. Rank, *Incestmotiv in Dichtung und Sage* and *Trauma der Geburt*.

already mentioned, even the time the foetus spends in its mother's womb has a libidinous character, and it is actually with the event of birth—the first and most distressing separation from the mother, the rupture of unity with her—that the Oedipus tragedy begins.[5] The libido, however, continues time and time again to be impelled toward the mother, sexualizing all her attentions and services; the activities of being nursed, being bathed, being helped with defecation, and so forth acquire a sexual coloration for the child. Here, too, are involved inevitable contacts with the various erogenous zones and the genitals that cause the child to experience pleasurable feelings and even sometimes his first erection. The child is drawn to his mother's bed, clings to his mother's body, and some obscure memory in his organism impels him to his mother's uterus, to return to that uterus. In this way the child is *organically* impelled toward *incest*. The situation is such that incestuous desires, feelings, and presentations are inevitably bound to arise.

In the course of these attractions of the little Oedipus to his mother, the *father* becomes the rival who incurs the hatred of his son. The father, after all, interferes with the child's relationship with his mother: He keeps the child from being taken into her bed, he forces the child to be self-reliant, to do without his mother's help, and so on. From this arises the child's infantile wish for the father's death, a death that would allow him to take undivided possession of the mother. Since the pleasure principle reigns supreme in the child's psyche at this stage of development, there is no limit to the production of both *incestuous* and *hostile* tendencies and desires and the images associated with them.[6]

When the reality principle comes into force and the father's voice, with all its prohibitions, begins gradually to transform into the voice of the child's own conscience, an onerous and relentless struggle with these incestuous impulses begins and they are repressed into the unconscious. The entire Oedipus complex is subjected to full amnesia. *Fear and shame* are engendered in place of the repressed impulses; they are brought about in the psyche by the very idea of the possibility of sexual impulses toward one's mother. The censorship has done a splendid job: The legal—the "official"—conscious protests with complete sincerity against the mere suggestion of the possibility of the Oedipus complex.

The Oedipus complex, according to Freud, does not by any means always pass through the process of repression without painful consequences for the child. It frequently leads to nervous disorders, in particular various infantile phobias.[7]

For Freud the concept of the Oedipus complex makes fully comprehensible why *myths* about incest, about the murder of a father by his son or, conversely,

---

[5] Rank, *Trauma der Geburt.*

[6] The same is applicable, with relations reversed, to a female child.

[7] See Freud, "Geschichte der Fobie eines 5-jährigen Knaben," in *Kleine Schriften zur Neurosenlehre*, Part 3.

about a father murdering his children, and other related legends are so widespread among so many different peoples. It also explains the overwhelming impression that Sophocles' famous tragedy makes on all of us, despite the fact that, from the point of view of the official conscious, we are bound to regard the Oedipus plot as a poetic fiction and a situation not in the least *typical* of human life. But this tragedy, Freud maintains, just as *any other great work of art, appeals not to our official conscious but to the whole of our psyche, above all, to the deepest levels of our unconscious.*[8]

The Oedipus complex, this first, prehistoric event in human life, has, according to Freud's theory, enormous, direct, and decisive significance for that life. This first love and first hate will always remain the most integrally organic feelings in a man's life. In comparison with these feelings all subsequent erotic relations, relations occurring in the light of consciousness, will amount to superficial and cerebral experiences, experiences that do not engage *the very depths of the organism and the psyche.* Rank and Ferenczi outrightly consider all of a man's subsequent love relations only a surrogate for his first, Oedipal love—a love that had been preceded by complete organic unity with its object, the mother. Future coitus is only a partial compensation for the lost paradise of the intrauterine state. All events in adult life borrow their psychical power from this first event that has been repressed into the unconscious—the Oedipus complex. In his later life a man will, without of course being in the least aware of it himself, reenact this aboriginal event of the Oedipus complex time and time again with the new partners in his life, transferring to them his repressed and, hence, eternally alive feelings toward his mother and father. The basis for this process is the so-called transference mechanism (*Übertragung*).

The transference mechanism is a very important point in psychoanalytical theory and practice. Freud understands it as *the unconscious displacement of repressed instincts*—principally sexual—*from their direct object to another, substitute object.* So, for example, during psychoanalytical treatment, the patient's attraction to his mother and enmity toward his father are usually transferred to the doctor, and in this way they are partially lived out. Therein lies the significance of transference for the practice of psychotherapy. Transference is one of the ways of *bypassing* the prohibitions of the official conscious and, even if only partially, of giving the unconscious a chance to come into its own and express itself.

Freud maintains that a man's love life depends in many respects on the degree of his success in freeing his libido from its attraction to his mother. *The first object of juvenile infatuation usually resembles the mother.*

---

[8] Psychological investigations of the type that use a psychoanalytical base in the endeavor to penetrate the depths of the human psyche (the region of the unconscious) have acquired in psychoanalytical literature the new term "depth psychology" (*Tiefenpsychologie*). [*Editor's note*]

However, the image of the mother may also play a disastrous role in the development of the sexual instinct. Fear of incest can, for the official conscious, render love of mother into an expressly spiritual kind of love—so-called respectful love—which is incompatible with even the idea of sensuality, and this fear can, moreover, form bonds in a man's psyche with any kind of respect, any kind of spirituality. Often this makes sexual intercourse with a woman one loves and respects impossible and leads to a fatal split of the unitary sexual instinct into two separate currents—sensual passion and spiritual attachment—which cannot join together in one and the same object.[9]

The Oedipus complex and everything associated with it comprise the main content of the unconscious system. Other, lesser sets of repressed psychical formations tie into the Oedipus complex throughout the entire course of a person's life. Culture and the individual's cultural growth require ever fresher repressions. But on the whole, *the bulk, the so-to-speak basic fund of the unconscious is comprised of infantile impulses that are sexual in character.* Of the "ego instincts," mention need be made only of the so-called *aggressive* impulses. In the infantile psyche, with its "all is permitted," these aggressive impulses appear full-blown: A child rarely wishes his enemies anything less than death. Such "mental murders" of persons, including even those closest to the child, amass in quantity during the first years of the child's life. They are all repressed into the unconscious later on. Owing to the predominance of the pleasure principle, the child is in all respects a pure and thoroughgoing egotist. This egotism knows no bounds, whether moral or cultural. A fair amount of material for the unconscious is produced on these grounds, as well.

Such, in terms of basic features, is the content of the unconscious. It can be summed up in the following formulaic statement: The world of the unconscious takes in everything that the organism might have done, had it been given over to the pleasure principle pure and simple and not been bound by the reality principle and culture. Thus, into the unconscious passes everything the organism really desired and had vivid presentations of (but satisfied to an insignificant degree) in the earliest, infantile stage of life when the pressure of the reality principle and of culture was still weak and when, moreover, the manifestations of a human's innate, organic self-centeredness were freer.

All of the above definitions and characterizations of the basic factors in Freud's conception of the unconscious—the pleasure and reality principles, repression, censorship, the theory of instincts, and, finally, the content of the unconscious—were worked out by Freud, as already noted, during the second and most positive period in the development of psychoanalysis. We in fact relied primarily on the works of that period for our exposition.

[9] Freud, "Zur Psychologie des Liebesleben," in *Kleine Schrifter zur Neurosenlehre*, Part 4.

However, we know that this theory of Freud's underwent quite substantial changes and expansions in the third period of development. We are also aware of the direction these changes took.

We shall not stop to consider in detail the whole set of new features that the third period brought in. After all, the culmination point of its development is in the offing only now, at the very time this is being written. Meanwhile, there is quite a lot about this period that has not yet taken definitive shape or reached final resolution. Both of Freud's books especially characteristic of this period suffer from inconclusiveness and, here and there, obscurity, differing in these respects from the almost classical lucidity, precision, and definitiveness of his earlier works. Therefore, we shall limit ourselves to a brief review of only what is of greatest importance.

The theory of instincts has undergone substantial changes. Instead of the earlier division into sexual instincts (continuation of the species) and ego instincts (preservation of the individual), a new binary division has appeared: (1) the *sexual instinct, or Eros,* and (2) *the death instinct.* The ego instinct, above all the idea of self-preservation, has been consigned to the sexual instinct (Eros), which thus has undergone considerable conceptual expansion, encompassing both sections of the earlier division.

By *Eros* Freud means the *instinct striving toward organic life,* toward its preservation and development at whatever cost, whether in terms of the continuation of the species (sexuality in the narrow sense) or preservation of the individual. *The death instinct* is understood as *aiming toward the return of all living organisms to the lifeless state of inorganic, inanimate matter*—a striving away from the exigencies of life and Eros.

All life, Freud maintains, is conflict and compromise between these two strivings. Every cell of a living organism contains the combination of both kinds of instincts—Eros and Death; to the one and the other, respectively, correspond the physiological processes of construction (anabolism) and destruction (catabolism) of living matter. As long as a cell is alive, Eros is dominant.

When the restless, life-oriented Eros finds satisfaction in the sexual way, then Death begins to make itself heard. Hence, the resemblance between the post-coital state and dying, and for certain lower animals the coincidence of the act of fertilization with actual death. The latter die because, once Eros is stilled, the death instinct is completely free to operate and carries out its task.

In its biological aspect, this new theory of Freud's reflects the strong influence of the noted German biologist and neo-Darwinian, Weismann; in its philosophical aspect, the equally strong influence of Schopenhauer.

The second special feature of the third period of development that we shall deal with is the expansion of the content of the unconscious, its enrichment with qualitatively new and unique factors.

A dynamic conception of the unconscious as "the repressed" was characteristic of the second period. Freud dealt with that conception primarily in his psychiatric research,[10] and, indeed, technical psychiatric interests were predominant during that period. The repressed, consisting, as we have seen, largely of sexual instincts, was regarded as antagonistic toward the conscious "I"—the ego. Now, in his most recent book, Freud proposes that the whole region of the psyche not coinciding with the ego be called *"das Es"*—"the id." The id is that inner, shadowy, elemental force made up of appetites and impulses that we do sometimes very keenly feel within us and that stands in opposition to our rational persuasions and good will. The id is the passions; the ego, the intelligence and reason. In the id the pleasure principle reigns supreme; the ego is the vehicle for the reality principle. The id is, moreover, unconscious.

Up to now, when speaking of the unconscious, we have had to do exclusively with the id—repressed impulses are, after all, precisely its properties. Therefore, the entire unconscious had the appearance of something *lower*, something *dark and immoral*, whereas everything higher, moral, and rational coincided with the conscious. This view is invalid. It is not only the id that is unconscious. The ego, too, and the ego *in its highest sphere*, accommodates *a region of the unconscious*.

In point of fact, the process of repression, which issues from the ego, is unconscious, and the work of the censorship, which is carried out in the interests of the ego, is likewise unconscious. Thus, a significant area of the ego also turns out to be unconscious. This is the area on which Freud has focused his attention during the third period. It was discovered to be far broader, deeper, and more substantial than it had seemed at first. From what we know of the unconscious as the repressed, we might conclude that *a normal human being is far more immoral than he himself believes*. This conclusion is correct, but we must now add that the normal human being is also *far more moral than he knows*. "Human nature," Freud writes, "has a far greater extent, both for good and for evil, than it thinks it has—i.e., than its ego is aware of through conscious perception."[11]

This higher, unconscious region in the ego Freud termed the *superego* (*Ich-ideal*).

The superego is first and foremost that *censor* whose orders are carried out by the process of repression. Moreover, the superego makes its presence felt in a whole host of other very important phenomena of personal and cultural life. It comes out in an *unaccountable sense of guilt* that oppresses the minds of certain people. The conscious does not acknowledge this guilt; it struggles with the

---

[10] "Pathological research has directed our interest too exclusively to the repressed," Freud himself remarks in *Das Ich und das Es*. [English translation from *The Standard Edition of the Complete Psychological Works of Sigmund Freud* (hereafter cited as *Standard Edition*), ed. James Strachey (London: The Hogarth Press and the Institute of Psycho-Analysis, 24 volumes, 1953-1974), 19 (1961): 19. *Translator.*]

[11] *Standard Edition* 19:52.

feelings aroused but cannot overcome them. These feelings have played a major role in various manifestations of religious atrocities connected with the affliction of suffering on oneself (asceticism, self-flagellation, self-immolation and the like). Furthermore, among manifestations of the superego belong "sudden instigations of conscience," instances of unusual severity toward one's own self, self-contempt, melancholy, and so forth. In all these phenomena the conscious "I"—the ego—is compelled to submit to a force *emanating from the depths of the unconscious, but a force that is, at the same time, moral,* often even "hypermoral," to use Freud's own term.

How was that force formed in the human psyche? How did the superego come about?

To understand this requires acquainting ourselves with a special psychical mechanism called "identification." A person's attraction to another person may go in either of two directions: It may aim at possessing that other person (for example, the child during the Oedipal phase strives to possess his mother), but it may also cause the person to strive to identify himself with the other, to conform to him, to become just like him, to assimilate that other person into his self. This second tendency is precisely the child's attitude toward his father—he wants to be like his father, to copy him. This second kind of relationship to an object (person) outside oneself is, moreover, the older of the two; it is connected with the earliest, oral stage of child development and the development of the human species. In this phase, the child—and prehistoric man—knows no other way of approach to an object than to ingest it; whatever seems to him of value he immediately tries to put into his mouth and, in that way, introduce into his organism. The endeavor to imitate is, as it were, the psychical surrogate for the more ancient ingestion. In human life, identification sometimes replaces the normal endeavor to possess the object of one's love. So, for example, in a case of unsuccessful love, where possession of the love object is impossible, a person may assimilate the qualities of the loved one, become like and identify with the loved one.[12] *Identification also explains the emergence of the superego in the human psyche.*

Of greatest importance for the formation of the superego is identification with the father during the period of the Oedipus complex. Here the child assimilates the image of his father, including the latter's virility, threats, commands, prohibitions. From this originate the superego's harsh and severe tones, expressed in the commands of conscience, of duty, of the categorical imperative, and so on. "You must . . . !" first rings in a person's soul as the voice of the father of the Oedipus complex stage; it is repressed together with the Oedipus complex into the unconscious, from where it continues to make itself heard as the voice of inner authority, of duty, of the highest commands of conscience,

[12] See Freud, *Massenpsychologie und Ich-Analyse* (1921), pp. 68-77.

entirely independent of the ego. Later in life, the authority of teachers, of religion, of culture are added to the father's voice, but these influences are more superficial and conscious and, therefore, must themselves borrow power from the earlier self-identification of a person with his father and with his father's will. "The superego," Freud writes, "retains the character of the father, while the more powerful the Oedipus complex was and the more rapidly it succumbed to repression, the stricter will be the domination of the superego over the ego later on—in the form of conscience or perhaps of an unconscious sense of guilt."[13]

Such is Freud's doctrine on the superego.

In concluding this chapter, let us note that in his latest book Freud defines the unconscious as *nonverbal*; it converts into the preconscious (from which it can always proceed into the conscious) "through becoming connected with the word presentations corresponding to it."[14] Freud ascribes greater significance to this definition here than he had done in his earlier works. Nevertheless, even here it remains without further elaboration.

With this we conclude our characterization of the unconscious. We now know its origins and we know its content, but we still do not know the most important of all—what was the material and what were the methods, that is, the investigatory procedures, that Freud used in order to arrive at all this knowledge about the unconscious? Only the answer to that question can, after all, put us in a position to judge the scientific validity and reliability of all that knowledge. To that topic the next chapter is devoted.

[13] *Standard Edition* 19:34-35.
[14] There, too, Freud cites the earlier work where that definition was first given. [See *Standard Edition* 19:20. *Translator.*]

CHAPTER 5

The Psychoanalytical Method

Compromise formations. The method of free association. Interpretation of dreams. Neurotic symptoms. The psychopathology of everyday life.

When expositing the early Freudian concept of the unconscious, we emphasized that Freud had not found *direct and unmediated* access to the unconscious but had learned about it *through the conscious* of the patient himself. Exactly the same thing has to be said about his mature method. Indeed, here is what Freud himself says on this point in his latest book: "All our knowledge is invariably bound up with consciousness. We can come to know the unconscious only by making it conscious."[1]

Freud's *psychological method* boils down to an *interpretative analysis of conscious formations* of a special kind—ones that *allow of being traced back to their unconscious roots.*

What are these formations like?

As we already know, the unconscious is precluded from direct access to the conscious and to the preconscious, at the threshold of which the censorship operates. However, as we also know, all repressed impulses retain their energy and, therefore, constantly strive to break through into consciousness.

They can do this (only partially) with the help of *compromises and distortions* that deceive the censorship and circumvent its vigilance. This distortion and disguising of repressed impulses occurs, of course, in the region of the unconscious, and it is from there, once having deceived the censorship, that they penetrate into the conscious, where they remain unrecognized. It is here, in the conscious, that the investigator finds them and subjects them to analysis.

[1] *Standard Edition* 19:19.

All these compromise formations fall into one or the other of two sets:

1. *Pathological formations*—symptoms of hysteria, obsessions, phobias, and also such pathological phenomena of everyday life as the forgetting of names, slips of the tongue and pen, and the like;

2. *Normal formations*—dreams, myths, and the images of creative art, philosophical, social, and even political ideas, in fact, the whole domain of human *ideological creativity*.

The border between these two sets is fluid, so that it is often difficult to tell where the normal ends and the pathological begins.

Freud's most substantive research was devoted to *dreams*. The methods of interpretation he applied to dream imagery have become classical and standard procedures for psychoanalysis as a whole.

Freud distinguishes two factors in a dream: (1) its manifest content (*manifester Inhalt*)—the dream images, usually taken from random impressions of the immediately preceding day, that we easily remember and willingly speak about with other people; and (2) latent dream thoughts (*latente Traumgedanken*) that fear the light of consciousness and are artfully *disguised* in the images of the manifest content of the dream. The conscious often does not even suspect their existence.[2]

How does one delve down to those latent thoughts, that is, how does one *interpret* dreams?

For this purpose, Freud proposed the method of "free fantasizing" (*freie Einfälle*) or "free association" (*freie Assoziation*) apropos the manifest images of the dream under scrutiny. *Free rein must be given to the psyche and all the restraining and critical faculties of consciousness must be relaxed*; one must allow anything at all to come to mind, even the most outlandish thoughts and images that have no apparent relevance to the dream being analyzed; one must become completely *passive* and allow free access to whatever comes to consciousness, even if it seem senseless, meaningless, with no connection to the matter at hand; one must endeavor only to be attentive to whatever *involuntarily* arises in the psyche.

When we actually attempt to do this, we immediately become aware that our efforts meet with strong *resistance* on the part of our conscious; a kind of *inner protest* is generated against our interpreting our dream. This protest takes various forms. Now we feel that the manifest content of the dream is understandable enough as is and needs no explanation; now, on the contrary, we regard our dream as so absurd and ridiculous that it cannot possibly make any sense; finally, we take a critical attitude toward the thoughts and images that

[2] Freud, *Traumdeutung*. The latter are sometimes called "residues of the day" because of their relation with impressions while awake.

enter our mind and we suppress them the instant they arise as things accidental and unrelated to the dream. In other words, *we constantly strive to maintain and adhere to the point of view of the legal conscious*; we are reluctant to overstep the laws that govern the territory of our psyche's highest level.

In order to *delve into the latent thoughts* of a dream, *this stubborn resistance must be overcome.* It, this resistance, represents precisely that force which, in the capacity of the censorship, has distorted the true content (the latent thoughts) of our dream and transformed it into the dream's manifest images (manifest content). This force is what hampers our present efforts; it is the cause of our easily and rapidly forgetting dreams and is responsible for those involuntary distortions to which we subject dreams when we do remember them. But the fact the resistance is present is an important symptom. where there is resistance, there unquestionably also is a repressed unconscious impulse striving to break through into consciousness; that indeed is the reason why the force of resistance is mobilized. *Compromise formations*—in this case, the manifest images of the dream—are meant to substitute for the repressed impulse in the only form the censorship will allow.

When, finally, resistance in its many and various expressions has been overcome, the free thoughts and images that run through one's consciousness, random and disconnected as they may seem, constitute the links of a chain along which it is possible to reach down to the repressed impulse—the latent content of the dream. This content will turn out to be a disguised wish fulfillment, in the majority of cases but not exclusively,[3] of an erotic and often infantile erotic character. Manifest dream images, thus, turn out to be substitute presentations—*symbols*—for the objects of that wish or, at any rate, to have some bearing on the repressed impulse.

The laws for the formation of the symbols that replace the objects of a repressed impulse are very complex. Their governing aim comes down to a matter of maintaining some, even if only remote, *connection* with the repressed presentation, on the one hand, and, on the other, of assuming a shape that would be wholly *legal*, correct, and acceptable for the conscious. This is accomplished by merging several images into one composite image, by interpolating a series of intermediary images linked both with the repressed presentation and with the one given in the manifest content of the dream, by implementing images of exactly opposite meaning, by transferring emotions and affects from their actual objects to other, indifferent details of the dream, by turning affects into their opposites, and the like.

Such is the technique for the formation of dream symbols.

What significance do these substitute images, these dream symbols, have? What purpose is served by these compromises between the conscious and the

---

[3] See *Handwörterbuch der Sexualwissenschaft*, p. 616.

unconscious, the permissible and the impermissible (but always wished for)? They serve as *safety valves* for repressed impulses and allow the unconscious to be *partially lived out*, thereby cleansing the psyche of energies held in and pent up in its depths.

The creation of symbols is partial compensation for the denial of satisfaction, under pressure from the reality principle, of all the organism's impulses and desires. It is a partial liberation, in compromise form, from reality, a return to the infantile paradise with its "all is permitted" and its hallucinatory wish fulfillment. The biological state of the organism during sleep is itself a partial resumption of the intrauterine situation of the foetus. We—unconsciously, of course—reenact that state, we play out a return to our mother's womb. We are undressed, we curl up under the blanket, we draw our knees up, bend our neck—in short, we recreate the foetal position; our organism is sealed away from all outside stimuli and influences; finally, our dreams, as we have seen, partially restore the reign of the pleasure principle.

Let us elucidate all that we have said with an illustration of a dream analysis produced by Freud himself.

The dream in question belongs to a man who had lost his father some years before. Freud begins by describing the manifest content of the dream:

> *His father was dead but had been exhumed and looked bad. He had been living since then and the dreamer was doing all he could to prevent him noticing it.* (The dream then went on to other and apparently very remote matters.)
>
> His father was dead; we know that. His having been exhumed did not correspond to reality; and there was no question of reality in anything that followed. But the dreamer reported that after he had come away from his father's funeral, one of his teeth began to ache. He wanted to treat the tooth according to the precept of Jewish doctrine: "If thy tooth offend thee, pluck it out." And he went off to the dentist. But the dentist said: "One doesn't pluck out a tooth. One must have patience with it. I'll put something into it to kill it; come back in three days and I'll take it out."
>
> "That 'take out'," said the dreamer suddenly, "that's the exhuming!"
>
> Was the dreamer right about this? It only fits more or less, not completely; for the *tooth* was not taken out, but only something in it that had died. But inaccuracies of this kind can, on the evidence of other experiences, well be attributed to the dream work. If so, the dreamer had condensed his dead father and the tooth that had been killed but retained; he had fused them into a unity. No wonder, then, that something senseless emerged in the manifest dream, for, after all, not everything that was said about the tooth could fit his father. Where could there possibly be a *tertium comparationis* between the tooth and his father, to make the condensation possible?
>
> But no doubt he must have been right, for he went on to say that he knew that if one dreams of a tooth falling out it means that one is going to lose a member of one's family.
>
> This popular interpretation, as we know, is incorrect or at least is correct only in a scurrilous sense. We shall be all the more surprised to find the topic thus touched upon reappearing behind other portions of the dream's content.

The dreamer now began, without any further encouragement, to talk about his father's illness and death as well as about his relations with him. His father was ill for a long time, and the nursing and treatment had cost him (the son) a lot of money. Yet it was never too much, he was never impatient, he never wished that after all it might soon come to an end. He was proud of his truly Jewish filial piety towards his father, of his strict obedience to Jewish law. And here we are struck by a contradiction in the thoughts belonging to the dream. He had identified the tooth and his father. He wanted to proceed with the tooth in accordance with Jewish law, which commanded him to pluck it out if it caused him pain or offence. He also wanted to proceed with his father, too, in accordance with the precepts of the law, but in this case it commanded him to spare no expense or trouble, to take every burden on himself, and to allow no hostile intention to emerge against the object that was causing him pain. Would not the two attitudes have agreed much more convincingly if he had really developed feelings toward his sick father similar to those toward his sick tooth—that is, if he had wished that an early death would put an end to his unnecessary, painful, and costly existence?

I do not doubt that this was really his attitude toward his father during the tedious illness and that his boastful assurances of his filial piety were meant to distract him from these memories. Under such conditions, the death wish against a father is apt to become active and to hide itself under the mask of such sympathetic reflections as that "it would be a happy release for him." But please observe that here we have passed a barrier in the latent dream thoughts themselves. No doubt the first portion of them was unconscious only temporarily—that is, during the construction of the dream; but his hostile impulses against his father must have been permanently unconscious. They may have originated from scenes in his childhood and have occasionally slipped into consciousness, timidly and disguised, during his father's illness. We can assert this with greater certainty of other latent thoughts which have made unmistakable contributions to the content of the dream. Nothing, indeed, is to be discovered in the dream of his hostile impulses towards his father. But if we look for the roots of such hostility to a father in childhood, we shall recall that fear of a father is set up because, in the very earliest years, he opposes a boy's sexual activities, just as he is bound to do once more from social motives after the age of puberty. This relation to his father applies to our dreamer as well: His love for him included a fair admixture of awe and anxiety, which had their source in his having been early deterred by threats from sexual activity.

The remaining phrases in the manifest dream can be explained now in relation to the masturbation complex. "*He looked bad*" is indeed an allusion to another remark of the dentist's to the effect that it looks bad if one has lost a tooth in that part of the mouth; but it relates at the same time to the "looking bad" by which a young man at puberty betrays, or is afraid he betrays, his excessive sexual activity. It was not without relief to his own feelings that in the manifest content the dreamer displaced the "looking bad" from himself on to his father—one of the kinds of reversal by the dream work which is familiar to you. "*He had been living since then*" coincides with the wish to bring back to life as well as with the dentist's promise that the tooth would survive. The sentence "the dreamer was doing all he could *to prevent him (his father) noticing it*" is very subtly devised to mislead us into thinking that it should be completed by the words "that he was dead." The only completion, however, that makes sense comes once more from the masturbation complex; in that connection it is self-evident that the young man did all he could to conceal his sexual life from his father. And finally, remember that we must always interpret what are called "dreams with a dental stimulus" as relating to masturbation and the dreaded punishment for it.

You can see how this incomprehensible dream came about. It was done by producing a strange and misleading condensation, by disregarding all the thoughts that were in the centre of the latent-thought-process and by creating ambiguous substitutes for the deepest and chronologically most remote of these thoughts. [4]

That is how a psychoanalytical interpretation of a dream works. The method of free association makes it possible, in the given case, to bring to light all the intermediary formations—the ailing tooth and the need to have it extracted—that connect the manifest images of the dream—*the father exhumed from his grave*—with a repressed unconscious impulse—*the infantile wish to be rid of one's father*. The latent thoughts of this dream—hostility toward the father and the urge to get rid of him—are so disguised in the manifest images that the dream fully satisfies the strictest moral requirements of consciousness. In all likelihood, Freud's patient did not find it easy to concur with the kind of interpretation Freud gave his dream.

This dream is interesting for the fact that its latent thoughts (secret wishes) provided outlet for hostility toward the patient's father that had been pent up in the patient's unconscious throughout his entire life. The dream condensed unconscious hostile impulses belonging to three periods of his life—the period of the Oedipus complex, the period of puberty (masturbation complex), and, finally, the period of the father's illness and death. In any case, the analytical probe plumbed to the very bottom of the dream—the infantile impulses of the Oedipus complex.

Freud uses the same methods for the analysis of other types of compromise formations, as well, particularly for investigation of the *pathological symptoms* of various nervous disorders. In point of fact, Freud came to dream interpretation out of concern with psychiatric needs and in the effort to utilize dreams as symptoms. Even though dream analyses were the material on which the method was elaborated, refined, and perfected, the prime material for drawing conclusions about the unconscious and its content was, of course, symptoms of nervous disorders.

We cannot delve into that interesting but highly specialized area here. We shall limit ourselves to a few brief remarks about the psychiatric application of this method of Freud's.

At a session of psychoanalytical treatment, the patient is supposed to tell the doctor everything that comes to mind concerning the symptoms and circumstances of his illness. The main aim in this case, as in dream interpretation, is to *overcome the resistance* that the patient's conscious brings to bear. But that

[4] *Standard Edition* 15 (1963): 188-190.

resistance at the same time serves as an important clue to the doctor. Wherever it flares up with particular force, there must be the patient's "sore point," which should become the doctor's main target of attention. We already know the dictum: *where there is resistance, there is repression.* The doctor's task is to dig down to the *repressed complexes* in the patient's psyche, because the root of all nervous disorders consists in the unsuccessful repression of some especially strong infantile complex (most often, the Oedipus complex). Once the complex is discovered, it must be given a chance to "drain," so to speak, into the patient's consciousness. In order for this to happen, the patient must "accept" the complex and then, with the doctor's help, thoroughly "live it out," that is, transform the *unsuccessful involuntary repression (Verdrängung)* of the complex into a *conscious and reasoned judgement (Verurteilung)* about it. In this way a cure is effected.

The psychoanalytical method was also applied by Freud to a host of very common *phenomena of everyday life*—slips of the tongue and pen, the forgetting of words and names, and so forth. Under analysis, all of these turned out to be compromise formations of the same type as dreams and pathological symptoms. To such phenomena Freud devoted a book called *The Psychopathology of Everyday Life.* Let us now consider a few examples from this area.

The president of the Austrian parliament once opened a parliamentary session with the words: "Gentlemen, I recognize that a quorum is present and, therefore, I declare the meeting closed."

He, of course, meant to say "open." What is the explanation for this slip of the tongue? The meeting promised to be a disagreeable one for him, and deep down he would have wished it were already over. And so this wish—a wish, needless to say, that he himself would never have acknowledged—infiltrated the statement he was making and, independently of his will and consciousness, produced a distortion.

Another example:

In his inaugural lecture, a certain professor intended to say: "I am not able (*Ich bin nicht geeignet*) to apprise all the merits of my esteemed predecessor." Instead he declared: "I am not apt (*Ich bin nicht beneigt*) to apprise, etc." Thus, instead of "*nicht geeignet*" (not able) he mistakenly used the similar sounding "*nicht geneigt*" (not apt). A quite different meaning came out than intended, but it in fact expressed the unconscious enmity that the professor felt toward his predecessor.[5]

Similar processes occur in cases of forgetting words and names. When we try to remember some appellation we have forgotten, other names and ideas arise in our consciousness that have some relationship to the forgotten item. These

[5] [Both examples are also found in *Introductory Lectures on Psycho-Analysis* (*Standard Edition* 15:4041). *Translator.*]

names and ideas that arise involuntarily are analogous to the *substitute images of dreams.* With their help we can work back to what we have forgotten. In such cases it always turns out that the *reason for the forgetting was some disagreeable remembrance associated in our mind with the forgotten appellation.* Exactly that was what had "allured into oblivion" the perfectly innocent word or name. Here is one such instance as reported by Freud:

> On one occasion a stranger had invited me to drink some Italian wine with him, but when we were in the inn it turned out that he had forgotten the name of the wine which he intended to order because of his very agreeable recollections of it. From a quantity of substitute ideas of different kinds which came into his head in place of the forgotten name, I was able to infer that thoughts about someone called Hedwig had made him forget the name. And he not only confirmed the fact that he had first tasted this wine when he was with someone of that name, but with the help of this discovery he recalled the name of the wine. He was happily married at the present time and this Hedwig belonged to earlier days which he had no wish to remember.[6]

Thus, the same psychical dynamics of conflict and compromise between the conscious and the unconscious, with which we are already familiar, extends, according to Freud, into the area of the most trivial phenomena of everyday life.

A further area of application for the psychoanalytical method is that of ideological formations in the strict and proper sense—myths, art, philosophical ideas, social and political phenomena. Of this area we shall speak in the next chapter.

[6] *Standard Edition* 15:111-112.

CHAPTER 6

Freudian Philosophy of Culture

Culture and the unconscious. Myth and religion. Art. Forms of social life. The trauma of birth.

All ideological creativity, according to the Freudian doctrine, springs from the same *psycho-organic* roots as do dreams and pathological symptoms; absolutely all aspects of creativity—in terms of repertoire as well as form and content—can be traced back to these roots. Each factor in an ideological system is strictly *determined along psychobiological lines*. It is a compromise product of the struggle of forces within the organism, an index either of the equilibrium of these forces or of the predominance of one. Just as with any pathological symptom or obsession, an ideological construct draws its strength from the depths of the unconscious. It differs from pathological phenomena in that it involves *firmer and more steadfast* compromise agreements between the conscious and the unconscious, agreements that are equally advantageous to both sides and, consequently, beneficial for the human psyche.[1]

In the Freudian philosophy of culture we meet all the "psychical mechanisms" already familiar to us, so that we need not take up too much time in our examination of it.

The creation of *mythological images* is completely analogous to the "dreamwork." Myth is the collective dream of a community. The images in myths are substitute symbols of repressed unconscious instincts. Of especially great importance are the myths connected with the experience and repression of the Oedipus complex. The well-known Greek myth about Cronus devouring his children, and his castration and murder at the hands of Zeus, who was saved by

---

[1] C. Jung, one of Freud's disciples, demonstrated a number of amazing coincidences between the fantasies of a patient suffering from *Dementia praecox* and the myths of early man. [*Editor's note*]

his mother's hiding him for a time within her body (return to the mother's womb), is one of the most typical examples of the kind. The derivation of all the symbols of this myth from the Oedipus complex is perfectly obvious. To the same set of myths belong legends about combat between father and son that are so widespread among all peoples: the combat of Hilderbrand and Hadubrand in the Germanic sagas, of Rustem and Zorab in the Persian, of Il'ja Muromec and his son in the Russian—these are all variations on one and the same perennial theme, *the struggle for possession of the mother.*

Religious systems are considerably more complex. Here, along with repressed complexes of sexual instincts, a major role is played by the unconscious superego. It is the Oedipus complex once again that supplies the nurturing ground for the development of religious ideas and cults. Depending on which of the two factors in the Oedipus complex attains predominance in religious experience—*the mother's power of attraction or the father's prohibitions and will*—religions are classified by Freudianism into matriarchal or patriarchal subdivisions. Typical examples of the former are the oriental religions of Astarte, Baal, and so on. The purest expression of a patriarchal religion is Judaism, with its prohibitions, commandments and, what is more, its rite of circumcision (symbol of the prohibition imposed by the father on the incestuous impulses of the son).

Let us now turn to art.

Freud himself applied his method of interpreting dreams and symptoms mainly to the aesthetic phenomena of *jokes and wit.*[2]

The forms of jokes are governed by the same laws that provide the formal structure of dream images, that is, the laws for the formation of substitute presentations with the same mechanism for bypassing the legal conscious through such devices as coalescence of words or images, substitution of images, verbal ambiguity, transference of meaning from one level to another, displacement of emotions, and so on.

Jokes and witticisms have the tendency to *bypass reality*, to provide relief from the *seriousness of life*, and to secure an outlet for repressed infantile impulses, whether sexual or aggressive.

Sexual jokes are the offspring of obscenity and are engendered as its aesthetic substitute. But what is obscenity? Obscenity is a *surrogate* for sexual performance, sexual satisfaction. Obscenity necessarily involves a woman, that is, it is calculated on a woman's presence, whether real or imagined. Its intent is to induce a woman's sexual arousal. It is a technique of seduction. Saying the names of obscene objects is a surrogate for seeing them or displaying them or touching them. Decked out in the form of a joke, obscenity is better able to mask its true tendency, making it more acceptable for the cultural consciousness. A good joke

---

[2] Freud, *Der Witz und seiner Beziehung zum Unbewussten*, 3rd Edition (1921).

needs a listener; its aim is not only to bypass a prohibition but also to implicate the listener via laughter, to make the laughing listener an accomplice and, thereby, as it were, *socialize* the transgression.

In jokes of the aggressive sort, under cover of artistic form, free expression is given to *infantile hostility* toward any law, regulation, or national or social institution to which *the unconscious attitude toward the father and the father's authority* (*Oedipus complex*) or hostility toward any person not oneself (*infantile self-centeredness*) has been transferred.

Thus, a joke, too, is only a safety valve for pent-up energies in the unconscious; it, too, in the final analysis, serves the unconscious and is governed by it. The needs of the unconscious are what create the form and content of jokes.

No other works devoted specifically to the topic of art are found among Freud's own writings. It was Freud's students and disciples, especially Otto Rank, who pursued the study of this area further.

According to the Freudian writers on art, every artistic image always has reference to the unconscious but does so in a form that deceives and reassures the conscious. This deception is salutary. It enables certain common human complexes to be "lived out" without creating serious conflicts with the conscious.

Of particularly great importance for all forms of art are *erotic symbols.* Behind the most innocent-seeming and commonplace of artistic images some erotic object is always decipherable. An example from the field of Russian literature might be cited here. A certain Professor Ermakov of Moscow applied the psychoanalytical method to an interpretation of the famous story "Nose" by N. V. Gogol'. The nose in "Nose" turns out to be, according to Ermakov, a substitute symbol for the penis. Underlying the whole theme of the loss of one's nose and the particular motifs implementing that theme in the story is a complex closely associated with the Oedipus complex (in its father's threat aspect)—the *castration complex: fear of the loss of one's penis or one's sexual potency.*[3] Further examples we believe would be superfluous.

But it is not only from the unconscious "id" that art draws its powers; its source might also be the unconscious "superego." So, for instance, *unconscious feelings of guilt* (one of Dostoevskij's basic themes), the *imposition of severe ethical injunctions* (a basic motif of the later Tolstoj), and other related motifs emanating from the sphere of the superego can also feed into creative art, although, to be sure, such motifs find their greatest importance in philosophical constructs rather than art.

Thus, the entire content side of art derives from *premises in individual psychology*; it reflects the play of psychical forces in the individual human soul.

---

[3] I. D. Ermakov, *Očerki po psixologii gogolevskogo tvorčestva* [Essays in the Psychology of Gogol's Creative Art] (Moscow-Petrograd, 1923).

No room is left for the reflection of objective socioeconomic existence with its forces and conflicts. Wherever we do find images in art taken from the world of social and economic relations, we are to understand that these images, too, have significance only as substitutes—behind such images, as behind Major Kovalev's nose, invariably lurks somebody's erotic complex.

So far as the forms and techniques of art are concerned, psychoanalyists either pass over such issues in complete silence or they explain form in terms of the old principle of *the least expenditure of energy*. The formal in art is regarded as that which requires of the perceiver a minimal input of energy for a maximal result. This *principle of economy* (in a somewhat more sophisticated way, to be sure) was applied by Freud to the analysis of the technique of jokes and witticisms.

We must now briefly deal with the psychoanalytical theory of the *origin of social forms*. *Massenpsychologie und Ich-Analyse*, Freud's most recent book, is devoted to the fundamentals of this theory.

At the center of this whole psycho-sociological construct stand the already familiar identification mechanism and the superego.

We have seen that the superego (an aggregate of unconscious imperatives, calls to duty, conscience, and the like) is formed in the human psyche by way of identification *with the father* and other, *unpossessable* objects of a person's first love. The superego includes within its range of manifestations one important area of which we have not yet had occasion to speak. It is a common fact that a person in love, in most instances, is inclined to attribute to the object of his love all manner of virtues and perfections that the latter does not possess in reality. In such cases we say that a person is idealizing the object of his love. *The process of idealization is unconscious*; indeed, the lover himself is totally convinced that all these virtues do belong to the object and he does not so much as suspect the subjective nature of the process of idealization that is taking place within his own psyche. Furthermore, it is not only the object of sexual love, in the narrow sense, that can be idealized; we often also idealize our teachers, our superiors, our favorite writers and painters, exaggerating their good qualities and overlooking their faults. Moreover, we can even idealize an institution or an idea. In effect, the range of possibility for idealization is quite broad.

How does the psychical mechanism of idealization work? We might describe the idealization process as the reverse of the process of superego formation. In the latter case, we incorporate an object into ourselves, we enrich ourselves by its addition; in the former case, on the contrary, we *project into an object a part of ourselves, namely, our superego, and we enrich the object while impoverishing ourselves*. In cases of ordinary sexual infatuation this process rarely goes very far. But if we wholly expropriate our superego in the object's favor or, in other words, if we place the object in the superego's stead, we deprive ourselves of any possibility of counteracting the will and power of that object. Indeed, with what could we do so? It has taken the place of the superego—the place of our critical faculty and the place of our conscience! The will of such an authority is incontrovertible. It is in just such a manner that the power and authority of the leader, the priest, the state, the church are established.[4]

Thus, the voice of the father, which, internalized in the period of the Oedipus complex and become the inner voice of conscience, is now, by a reversed process, once again projected outward and becomes the voice of an external authority of an incontrovertible and sacrosanct character.

The very same process whereby one person's superego is replaced by the personality of another is what, according to Freud, underlies *hypnotic phenomena*, as well. The hypnotist appropriates the patient's superego and takes its place. From that position he easily controls the patient's weak conscious ego.

Needless to say, social organizations involve more than just this one-to-one relationship of an individual person to an authority figure—leader, priest, or other. Beside this relationship there is the fact of the *social solidarity* among all the members of a tribe, a church, a state. How is this fact to be explained? In Freud's view, it is to be explained by the same identification mechanism that we have already seen. Owing to the fact that all members of a tribe have transferred their superegos to one and the same object (the chief), they have no other course than to identify with one another and become equals, neutralizing their differences. That is how a tribe is formed.

Here is Freud's own summary definition: "A primary group . . . is a number of individuals who have substituted one and the same object for their ego ideal and have consequently identified themselves with one another in their egos."[5]

As the reader can see, Freud maintains that social organization is also wholly explainable in terms of psychical mechanisms. Psychical forces create human contacts, shape them, and give them solidity and durability. Meanwhile, conflicts with established social authority, social and political revolution, in most cases, have roots in the id—the id rebelling against the superego or, rather, rebelling against the external object standing in place of the superego. *The least significance in all areas of cultural creativity belongs to the conscious ego.* This ego adheres to the interests of reality (the external world) with which it attempts to reconcile the id's appetites and passions, while the superego, with its categorical demands, exerts its pressure on the ego from above. Thus, the conscious ego serves three mutually hostile masters—the external world, the id, and the superego—and endeavors to reconcile the conflicts that constantly arise among them. In cultural creativity the ego plays a *formal and constabulary role. The driving spirit, and the power and profundity, of culture are creations of the id and superego.*

[4] *Massenpsychologie und Ich-Analyse* (1921), Chapter 7.
[5] *Standard Edition* 18:116.

The tendencies inherent in the final stage of development of Freudianism have found their most extreme and acute expression, as already pointed out, in the book by Otto Rank called *The Trauma of Birth*. This book is something of a synthesis of Freudian philosophy of culture and to it we must turn in concluding our exposition of Freudianism.

It should be noted that Rank is Freud's favorite student and is considered the Freudian of greatest orthodoxy. His book is dedicated to his teacher and commemorates the latter's birthday. Under no circumstances can it be claimed as mere eccentricity. It expresses to the full the spirit of Freudianism today.

The entire life of a man and all his cultural creativity amount for Rank to nothing more or less than his *living out and overcoming, in various ways and with the help of various means, the trauma of birth*.

A man's birth into the world is traumatic. The organism, ejected from inside the mother's womb by the process of labor, experiences a terrible and excruciating shock the like of which will only come again with the shock of death. The horror and pain of the trauma are what initiated the human psyche; the trauma forms the bottom of the human soul. The terror of birth becomes the first experience to be repressed and the one onto which all subsequent repressions will be drawn from then on. The trauma of birth is the root of the unconscious and of the psychical in general. Throughout the rest of his life a man can never entirely be rid of the terror experienced at birth.

But together with this feeling of terror an urge to go back is engendered—an urge to return to the paradise experienced in the intrauterine state. This longing to return and this sense of horror constitute the basis for the ambivalent attitude that a person feels toward his mother's womb. It both attracts and repels. The "trauma of birth" determines the direction and meaning of personal life, and of cultural creativity, as well.

The *intrauterine state* is characterized by there being *no breach between need and its satisfaction*, that is, no breach between the *organism* and *its external reality*. Indeed, for the foetus there is no external world, properly speaking; its world is the mother's organism, which is a direct extension of its own organism. All the characteristic features of paradise and the Golden Age in myths and sagas, of the future world harmony of philosophical speculations and religious revelations and, finally, of the socioeconomic paradise of political utopias—all these clearly display unmistakable signs of their origin from that urge to return to the intrauterine life that all men once experienced. *All these notions have as their basis a vague, unconscious memory of a paradise that really did exist*, and that is why they exercise so powerful an effect on men's minds. They are not fictions, but their truth belongs not to the future but to every man's past. To be sure, the gates of paradise are guarded by a grim keeper—the terror of birth, which prevents that memory from being *fully awakened* and which causes the urge to return to the womb to be veiled in all manner of substitute images and symbols.

The trauma of birth appears in pathological symptoms: infantile phobias, adult neuroses and psychoses. It send shocks to the ill person's body, nonproductively repeating (in diminished form, to be sure) the actual shock experienced at the moment of birth. But the trauma is not lived out thereby. A genuine overcoming of this trauma is found only by way of cultural creativity. Rank defines culture as *the aggregate of efforts to transform the external world into a substitute, a surrogate (Ersatzbildung) of the mother's womb.*

All culture and industry are symbolic. We live in a world of symbols, all of which, in the final analysis, signify one thing—*the mother's womb* (more strictly, the uterus) and the accesses to it. What is the cave that primeval man sought refuge in? What is the room that we feel cosy in? What is homeland, state, etc.? They are all only surrogates for the mother's protective womb.

Rank has analyzed architectural forms and tries to prove their covert resemblance to the uterus. He derives the forms of art from the same source—the trauma of birth. So, for example, archaic statues that represent the human body in stooped or sitting postures unambiguously display the *foetal position*. Only the human being in Greek plastic art—the athlete at free play in the external world—signifies an overcoming of the trauma. The Greeks were the first to succeed in feeling at home in the external world; they were not drawn to the darkness and comfort of the intrauterine state. The Greeks had solved the riddle of the Sphinx, which was, according to Rank, none other than the riddle of human birth.

Thus, all creativity is conditioned, with respect to content as well as to form, by the act of birth into the world. However, by far the best surrogate of paradise, the fullest compensation for the trauma of birth, is, according to Rank, *sexual life. Coitus is a partial return to the womb.*

Death, Rank claims, is also preceived by man as a return to the womb. The fear associated with the thought of death repeats the terror of birth. The most ancient forms of burial—the hole dug in the ground ("Mother Earth"), the sitting position of the corpse with legs drawn up (foetal position), also burial in a boat (an allusion to the uterus and the amniotic fluid), the shape of the coffin, the rituals connected with burial—all these things reveal an unconscious conception of death as a return to the mother's womb. The Greek method of burning corpses again signifies the most successful overcoming of the trauma of birth. The final spasms of the death agony, as Rank sees it, exactly repeat the first spasms of the organism in the act of being born.

The methods Rank used in his work were completely subjective. He attempted no objective, physiological analysis of the trauma of birth and its possible effect on the subsequent life of the organism. He only sought to find reminiscences of the trauma in dreams, in pathological symptoms, in myths, art, and philosophy.

Highly characteristic of Rank's approach is his conception of the *psychoanalytical session* as a recapitulation of the act of birth (the very period of psychoanalytical treatment is normally about nine months). At the start, the patient's libido is focused on the doctor; the doctor's office is kept semi-dark (only the patient is located in the illuminated portion of it, the doctor sits in the half-light) and this represents the mother's womb for the patient. The end of treatment reproduces the trauma of birth. The patient is supposed to liberate himself from the doctor and, thereby, to work out his severance from his mother—all because the trauma of birth is the ultimate source of all nervous disorders.

With this we may conclude our exposition of Freudianism. Rank's book provides an excellent transition to the critical section of our study. It is a magnificent *reductio ad absurdum* of certain aspects of Freudianism.

PART III

A CRITICAL ANALYSIS
OF FREUDIANISM

CHAPTER 7

Freudianism as a Variant of Subjective Psychology

Freudianism and modern psychology. The elementary composition of the psyche and the unconscious. The subjectivism of the "dynamics" of the psyche. Critical analysis of the theory of erogenous zones. Freudianism and biology.

In our second chapter we characterized the two basic trends in modern psychology—the subjective and the objective. Now we must try to give an exact and detailed answer to the question regarding Freudianism's position with respect to those trends.[1]

Both Freud and his followers maintain that they have effected a radical reform of the old psychology and that through their efforts the foundation for an entirely new, objective science of psychology has been established.

Unfortunately, neither Freud nor any of his followers has ever made the slightest effort to elucidate precisely and concretely the Freudian position on contemporary psychology and its methods. The lack constitutes a major deficiency in Freudianism. The psychoanalytical school, after originally having been the target of unanimous persecution by the scientific community, withdrew into itself and adopted somewhat *sectarian modes* of operation and thought not altogether appropriate to scientific endeavors. It became the habit of Freud and his students to quote only themselves and refer only to one

---

[1] The critical literature on Freud is small. In addition to works already cited, let us mention Maag, "Geschlectsleben und seelische Störungen," in *Beiträge zur Kritik der Psychoanalyse* (1924); Otto Hinrichsen, *Sexualität und Dichtung* (1912); Edgar Michaelis, "Die Menschheits-Problematik der Freudschen Psychoanalyse," in *Urbild und Maske* (Leipzig, 1925).

another. In more recent times, they have begun quoting from Schopenhauer and Nietzsche, as well. The rest of the world hardly even exists for them.[2]

We repeat, Freud never made any serious attempt to delineate his doctrine with respect to other psychological trends and methods in concrete and detailed terms. Thus, we have no clear idea of his position with regard to the *introspective method*, the *laboratory-experimental method*, the *Wurtzburg school* (Messer and others), *functional psychology* (Stumpf and others), *differential psychology* (W. Stern)[3] and more recent attempts at creating *objective methods* by the school of so-called American behaviorism. Nor was Freud's position ever made clear concerning the famous controversy over *psychophysical parallelism versus psychophysical causality* that so aroused the psychologists and philosophers of his generation.[4]

Whenever Freud and his students contrast their conception of the psychical to all other psychology—without, alas, even troubling themselves to differentiate that "other psychology"—they bring one accusation to bear against it: *its identification of the psychical with the conscious*. For psychoanalysis, in contrast, the conscious is but one of the psychical systems.

Is it, perhaps, that the difference between psychoanalysis and all other psychology is really so great that there can be nothing in common between them, not even that minimum of common language essential for comparison and delimitation? Freud and his students apparently are convinced that this is so.

But is it?

The fact of the matter is that *Freudianism transferred into its constructs all the fundamental defects of the subjective psychology of the time*. There is no difficulty ascertaining this fact, provided only we not let ourselves be misled by the sectarian but still, on the whole, impressive and apt terminology of the doctrine.

In the first place, Freudianism dogmatically appropriated the old categorization of mental phenomena—originating with J.-C. Tetens and made a philo-

---

[2] It must be said that official science up to the present time has still not fully legitimized Freudianism, while in academic circles it is even considered bad taste to talk about it. See, Wittels, *S. Freud, der Mann, die Schale, die Lehre* (1924). In Willie Moog's survey of German philosophy in the twentieth century (1923), Freud and psychoanalysis are not mentioned at all. In Müller-Freienfels's survey, there is only passing mention contained in a few lines.

[3] All of these were factions of subjective psychology contemporary with the first and second periods in the development of Freudianism.

[4] Freud himself does acknowledge psychophysical causality, but, at the same time, he displays the traits of a parallelist at every step of the way. Moreover, his entire method is based on the hidden, never articulated assumption that for everything somatic one could find corresponding psychical equivalents (in the unconscious psyche) and, consequently, it is possible to dispense with the somatic in and of itself and deal exclusively with its psychical counterparts.

sophical truism thanks to Kant—into Will (desires, drives), Feeling (emotions, affects) and Mind (sensations, presentations, thoughts). Moreover, it retains exactly the same definitions of these faculties as were in common use by the psychology of the time and, as we see, exactly the same differentiation among them. Indeed, if we take a look at the *elementary makeup* of the psyche, as Freudianism conceives of it, we find that it is composed of sensations, presentations, desires, and feelings, that is, of exactly those same elements out of which the old psychology had built the "mental life" of man. What is more, without the slightest critical qualification and, moreover, in their usual, then current meanings, all these psychical elements are transferred by Freud to the domain of the unconscious. In the unconscious, too, we find desires, feelings, presentations.

But these elements of psychical life, after all, exist only *for consciousness*. And the old psychology had produced its breakdown of the psyche into elementary components with the aid of the usual method of introspection, a method that, in its usual form, cannot take us beyond the confines of the "official conscious," as Freud himself asserts.

Introspection is indeed a thoroughly conscious process. Even the subjectivist psychologists, in the persons of some of their most eminent representatives, and a good deal before Freud, argued that introspection was not impartial (could not rid itself of value judgements), on the one hand, and, on the other, tended to *overrationalize* psychical life, and that, therefore, its evidence required substantial revision. In any case, introspection is possible only from a conscious point of view. The old psychology knew no other point of view and that is why it identified the psychical with the conscious.

Thus, it is clear that the breakdown of the psyche into the elements of feeling, will, and mind was dictated to the old psychology by none other than consciousness. The point of view of consciousness set the guidelines for laying down all the bases of subjective psychology.

But have we any right to construct the unconscious on analogy with the conscious and to assume that it contains exactly the same elements as we find in the conscious? Nothing gives us that right. Once consciousness is cast aside, it becomes totally senseless to retain feelings, presentations, and desires.

When a person self-consciously motivates his own actions, he can hardly help, of course, but refer to his feelings, desires, and presentations; but once we start analyzing those actions objectively, endeavoring to adhere consistently and throughout to the point of view of external apprehension, we shall find no such elements anywhere in the makeup of behavior. External, objective apprehension has to rely on different—*material*—elementary components of behavior, components that have nothing in common with desires, feelings, and presentations.

Thus, only in the light of subjective consciousness does the picture of our psychical life appear to us one of conflict of feelings, desires, and presentations.

Whatever real, objective forces might underlie that conflict, our self-consciousness can tell us nothing at all about it. If we attach the label "unconscious" to certain desires and feelings and the labels "preconscious" and "conscious" to others, we merely lapse into inner contradiction with ourselves but do not step out beyond the confines of subjective consciousness and the picture of psychical life open to it. Once the self-conscious point of view is cast aside, the whole of that picture and all of its component parts must also be rejected and a wholly different point of departure has to be sought for a conception of the psyche. That is exactly what objective psychology is doing. Freud, on the other hand, has tried erecting a completely new, quasi-objective edifice of the human psyche out of the old subjectivist bricks. What, after all, is "unconscious desire" if not the same old brick only turned around?

But Freudianism does even worse things than that. It not only transfers elements of the conscious to the unconscious, it *preserves fully intact in the unconscious the specific differences and logical distinctions of all these elements.* The unconscious turns out to be, if we follow Freud, a vivid and diverse world where all presentations and images correspond with perfect accuracy to specific referents, where all desires are specifically oriented and all feelings retain their entire wealth of nuances and delicate transitions.

Let us turn attention to the operation of the censorship. Freud considers the censorship a "mechanism" that operates completely *unconsciously* (the conscious, as the reader will recall, not only does not control the work of the censorship but does not even suspect its existence). Yet, how delicately this "unconscious mechanism" detects all the logical subtleties of thoughts and all the moral nuances of feelings! The censorship exhibits enormous ideological erudition and refinement; it makes purely logical, ethical, and aesthetic selections among experiences. Can this possibly be compatible with its unconscious, *mechanical* structure?

All of Freud's other "psychical mechanisms" display exactly the same supremely "conscious" and ideological character (for example, the transference mechanism that the reader now knows so well). Actually, the quality of a "mechanism" is what they have least of all. They belong not at all to the realm of physical nature; they are not naturalistic but *ideological.*

The concept of the unconscious, therefore, does not move the psyche the slightest bit closer to material nature; its implementation does not in the least help us connect a psychical system of laws with the objective system of laws for nature in general. The rift between the inner-subjective sphere and the material sphere remains exactly the same in psychoanalysis as in the psychology of consciousness.

Needless to say, all those methodological difficulties that inevitably accompany a breach in the integrity and consistency of external apprehension arise also in the case of Freudianism. Having taken a subjective position, psychoanalysis has deprived itself of a direct and unmediated approach to the material world.

It can have nothing to do with that world and must either ignore it altogether or dissolve it in the psychical world.

Freud and his students nowhere in fact deal *directly* with the material composition and material processes of the bodily organism; they look only for somatic reflections in the psyche, that is, in the final analysis, they also subordinate everything organic to the methods of introspection—they psychologize the organic.

Just such *psychologization of the somatic* is egregiously exhibited in Freud's doctrine on the erogenous zones. Freud makes no provision for a physiological theory of the erogenous zones, he takes no stock whatever of their chemistry or their physiological relationship with other parts of the body. It is only their psychical equivalents that he subjects to analysis and investigation, that is, he focuses attention on the role played by subjective presentations and desires, associated with the erogenous zones, in the psychical life of a human individual and from that individual's inner, introspective point of view.

The position and function in the total organization of the body of this or that erogenous zone (for example, the genitals)—the internal secretion of the sex glands, its influence on the operation and form of other organs, its relationship with the constitution of the body, and so on—all these processes, detectable in the external material world, are left completely undefined by Freud and in no real sense even taken into account.

How the role of an erogenous zone in the material composition of the body connects with the role it plays in the subjective psyche, taken in isolation, is a question for which Freud provides us no answer. As a result, we are presented with a kind of duplication of erogenous zones: *What happens with erogenous zones in the psyche becomes something completely separate and independent of what happens with them physically, chemically, and biologically in the material organism.*

These features of psychoanalysis take on particularly bold relief when Freud attempts to construct a theory of human character types on the basis of the erogenous zones doctrine. We shall mention here only one of the points in the theory that most acutely reveals its subjectivism.

Freud claims that the predominance of the anal zone in infantile eroticism leads to the development of specific character traits that will stay with a person throughout his life. Thus, the anal erotic develops the traits of frugality and parsimony and does so in the following way. The infant's fondness for holding back feces and prolonging the excretory act in order to achieve maximal pleasure from its performance is transformed in the adult (whose anal eroticism has been subjected to repression and has become unconscious) into a passion for holding onto and hoarding gold (money), which bears a resemblance to feces.

There is not a single word in this theory about any of the material bases of character formation that are inherent in the constitution of the body or about the physical or objective social effects of the environment. *The entire process of character formation runs its course within the confines of the subjective psyche viewed as an isolated entity.* Between holding back feces and holding onto money, between feces and gold, there is only the most farfetched, subjective resemblance, but there are no real, no material connections that might bind them together in the material composition of the organism itself or in the environment, that is, there is nothing to support that resemblance in objective apprehension. Thus, in Freud's way of looking at it, the erogenous zones determine a person's character and behavior (for, after all, a person's character is wholly inseparable from its expression in his behavior) *in complete disassociation from the body, the bodily constitution, and, in general, from any kind of material environment.*

That Freud should take such an attitude toward the material composition of the organism is wholly understandable. Inner experience, extracted by means of introspection, cannot in fact be directly linked with the data of objective, external apprehension. To maintain a thorough consistency only the one or the other point of view can be pursued. Freud has ultimately favored the consistent pursuit of the inner, subjective point of view; all external reality is for him, in the final analysis, merely the "reality principle," a principle that he places *on the same level* with the "pleasure principle."

Certain Freudians (Rank, Pfister, Groddeck) claim that psychoanalysis has succeeded in detecting a wholly unique realm of being, a realm neither of physical being nor of psychical being but of *neutral* being, as it were, out of which, by way of differentiation, both physical and psychical being can subsequently emerge.

It is to this kind of neutral being that the deepest levels of the unconcious belong; only at its very highest levels—those closest to the preconscious—does differentiation between mind and body begin to take place.

Such an assertion on the part of the Freudians mentioned is, of course, philosophically naive in the extreme. It completely bypasses the *question of method*, a question, in this instance, of decisive importance.

We might ask: In the purview of which kind of apprehension—internal or external—is this neutral being present and does its process of differentiation occur?

The Freudians mentioned studiously avoid this question. But we know that we shall find no being of this sort in the purview of external apprehension. There we find *a process of the extreme complication of organized matter* that leads, at some specific point, to the manifestation of the psyche as a *new quality of that matter.* But of course nowhere in the purview of external apprehension do we ever find the issuance of matter and psyche from some third thing. We have to do here with a naive metaphysical assertion that draws its material from internal, subjective apprehension but decks it out in a fictitious neutral form.

Certain partisans of Freud claim, having primarily his "theory of instincts" in mind, that psychoanalysis has its objective basis in biology.

This claim is completely groundless. One can with greater right speak of Freud's psychologization and subjectivization of biology. Freud dissolves all objective biological forms and organismic processes in the subjective-psychical. All those biological terms, with which the pages of psychoanalytical books teem, lose their objective rigor, so thoroughly dissolved are they in the subjective-psychological context.

To substantiate this point we need only cite Freud's classification of instincts.

All instincts other than the sexual are lumped together by Freud into the one set of *ego instincts*—the *Ich-triebe*. The flagrantly subjectivist principle of this classification is perfectly clear. It hardly need be said that such a classification is inadmissible from the rigorous biological point of view. Even the vitalists, extreme as they are, have never openly acknowledged a belief that biology could have anything to do with "I."

As for Freud's second, revised classification of instincts (that of the third period), it has taken on an overtly metaphysical character. Eros, stripped of any specific somatic source and extended to cover all manifestations of organic life without exception, is in no way superior to Bergson's "élan vital" or Schopenhauer's "Will"; and the death instinct is in no way superior to gravitation toward Nirvana.

Thus, *psychoanalysis in every respect faithfully adheres to the point of view of internal, subjective apprehension*. Viewed in terms of fundamental methodology, it does not differ in any essential way from the psychology of consciousness. It is another species of subjective psychology and nothing more. In the final analysis, psychoanalysis, too, relies on the data of introspection. To be sure, it gives these data a different interpretation—it attempts to build them into a different picture of the human psyche. But no matter how you interpret subjective data, if you remain on the grounds of internal apprehension, you will still get nothing objective out of them. In order to do so, you must change the point of view itself. That precisely is what Freud has not done.

CHAPTER 8

The Dynamics of the Psyche
as a Struggle of Ideological Motives
and Not of Natural Forces

The novelty of Freudianism. The dynamics of the psyche as a struggle of motives. The projection of social dynamics into the individual. The projection of the conscious present into the unconscious past. Facts and constructs. The objective factors of the dynamics of the psyche.

We have now ascertained that Freudianism is merely one species of subjective psychology. We have also seen wherein consists the common ground upon which Freudianism and all other subjectivist doctrines converge. But the issue is not exhausted thereby; we must also make a clear-cut delimitation and proper assessment of what it is precisely that *distinguishes Freudianism* from other subjectivist trends.

For, indeed, there is something paradoxically novel and original about Freudianism that strikes every newcomer to the doctrine. This impression of novelty most likely also formed in our reader's mind as he followed our exposition of psychoanalysis. This is something we must look into.

What immediately strikes one upon first acquaintance with Freud's doctrine and what remains the final and strongest impression of the entire construction is, of course, the *strife*, the *chaos*, the *adversity* of our psychical life running conspicuously throughout Freud's whole conception and which he himself referred to as the "dynamics" of the psyche.

In this respect Freudianism is really quite different than all other psychological trends. Mental life for the old psychology was all "peace and quiet": everything put right, everything in its place, no crises, no catastrophes; from birth to death a smooth, straight path of steady and purposive progress, of gradual mental growth, with the adult's consciousness of mind coming to replace the child's innocence. This naive *psychological optimism* is a characteristic feature of all pre-Freudian psychology. The only difference was that in some cases this optimism was expressed explicitly, while in others it permeated the whole picture of human mental life in more covert form.

This psychological optimism was the legacy of the *biological optimism* that reigned in science before Darwin. It amounted to the naive notion of the omniscient purposiveness of the living organism, a notion finally replaced by the Darwinian doctrine on the struggle for existence, the extinction of the weak, and the survival and propagation of only the fittest minority. A strict concept of natural necessity came to prevail in all domains of post-Darwinian biology. Only the psyche, governed by perspicacious consciousness, remained as the last refuge for the concepts of purposiveness, harmony, and so on, that had been expelled from all other fields. The psychical stood as the realm of harmony and order in opposition to the natural and the elemental.

To all appearances, Freudianism did produce a most radical change in these views on the psyche.

The human psyche belongs to the realm of nature, human psychical life is part of elemental life—that above all was the message the public at large seized upon out of the entire doctrine of Freud. Those people inclined toward Nietzscheanism (and there were quite a few of them among Freud's admirers) preferred to speak rather of the "tragicness of psychical life."

Apropos the last point, it should immediately be noted that while natural necessity is certainly a stranger to purposiveness and harmony, it is no less remote from tragedy. However, perhaps that expression ought not to be taken as characterizing Freudianism as a whole.

Now, did Freud really succeed in detecting Nature in our psyche? Are the conflicts of the "ego," "id," and "superego," the "death instinct" and "Eros" really the conflicts of elemental forces? Or are they perhaps only conflicts of motives in the individual human consciousness? If that is the case, then we have something more like a "storm in a teacup" than a conflict of elemental forces.

In order to answer this question, it behooves us to restate in a somewhat different connection a set of ideas that we began to develop in the preceding chapter.

Freud's whole psychological construct is based fundamentally on human verbal utterances; it is nothing but a special kind of interpretation of utterances. All these utterances are, of course, constructed in the *conscious sphere of the psyche*. To be sure, Freud distrusts the surface motives of consciousness; he tries instead to penetrate to deeper levels of the psychical realm. Nevertheless, Freud does not take utterances in their objective aspect, does not seek out their physiological or social roots; instead he attempts to find the true motives of behavior in the utterances themselves—the patient is himself supposed to provide him information about the depths of the "unconscious."

Thus, Freud's construct remains within the confines of what a person himself can say about himself and his behavior on the basis of his own internal apprehension. Freud, to be sure, directs introspection along new pathways, makes it penetrate other levels of the psyche, but *he does not relinquish introspection as the sole method of authenticating the reality of psychical events.* The "unconscious," too, can and should be included in the sphere of introspection. After all, the patient is himself supposed to recognize the content of the "unconscious" (some repressed complex, for instance), to recall it, to attest to its existence with the aid of introspection. It is only in this way that a repressed "unconscious" experience acquires the value of a psychological fact.

For introspection, all the products of the unconscious take the forms of desires or impulses, find *verbal* expression and in *that* shape, that is, in the shape of a *motive*, enter into a person's awareness.

It is completely understandable that, in Freud's doctrine, the interrelations prevailing between the conscious and the unconscious should be so thoroughly unlike the relations between two *material* forces that allow of a precise objective account. Indeed, Freud's "conscious" and "unconscious" are ever at odds; between them prevail mutual hostility and incomprehension and the endeavor to deceive one another. Surely interrelations of this sort are only possible between two ideas, two ideological trends, two antagonistic persons, and not between two natural, material forces! Is it conceivable, for instance, that two natural forces engage in mutual deception or mutual nonrecognition?

Of course, only after entering into consciousness and donning the forms of consciousness (the forms of desires, thoughts, etc. with specific content) can products of the unconscious engage in conflict with ethical precepts or be perceived as deception of the "censorship."

Thus, *the whole of Freud's psychical "dynamics" is given in the ideological illumination of consciousness.* Consequently, *it is not a dynamics of psychical forces but only a dynamics of various motives of consciousness.*

In the whole Freudian construct of a psychical conflict, together with all the mechanisms through which it operates, we hear only the biased voice of the subjective consciousness interpreting human behavior. The unconscious is nothing but one of the motives of that consciousness, one of its devices for interpreting behavior ideologically.

What is the consciousness of an individual human being if not the ideology of his behavior? In this respect we may certainly compare it with ideology in the strict sense—as the expression of class consciousness. But no ideology, whether of person or class, can be taken at its face value or at its word. An ideology will lead astray anyone who is incapable of penetrating beyond it into the hidden play of objective material forces that underlies it.

For instance, a religious creed deludes only a person who believes in it and naively takes it for what it claims itself to be. But for the Marxist historian this same creed may present an extremely important and valuable document faithfully reflecting certain social contradictions and interests of specific groups of people. He can bring to light the real economic and social conditions that inevitably gave rise to the religious creed in question.

That is how the objectivist psychologist works. He does not take verbal utterances on trust—or any motivation or explanation that a person himself, on the basis of his own inner apprehension, might give his behavior. He tries to discover the objective roots not only of a person's behavior as a whole but of his verbal utterances, as well. No longer will these utterances be able to lead him astray. They will be for him an accurate expression of objective conditions of behavior—physiological and socioeconomic conditions. Behind the "dynamics" of the psyche, behind the conflict of motives, the objectivist psychologist reveals the material dialectics of nature and history.

That is not how Freud works. Freud lets himself be drawn into the conflict of subjective motivations of consciousness. The fact that he prefers a special set of motives—unconscious ones—and extracts such motives in a special way does not change matters in the least. A motive remains a motive—it does not acquire the weight of a material phenomenon. Freud's system provides us no access to the fertile grounds of objective apprehension.

But where do all those "forces" with which Freud populates the psyche come from—the "ego," "the id," the "superego" and so forth?

The conflict of motives supplies no evidential grounds for these forces. The conflict of motives is a real phenomenon accessible to objective apprehension—after all, it finds expression in verbal utterances. Psychical forces, on the contrary, are arbitrary constructs that Freud utilizes in the effort to explain that conflict. As is true of the majority of constructs in subjective psychology, Freud's theory is a "projection" of certain objective relations of the external world into the world of the psyche. What finds expression there is, in the very first instance, the extremely complex *social interrelationship between doctor and patient*.

In what does this interrelationship consist?

A patient wishes to hide from the doctor certain of his experiences and certain events of his life. He wants to foist on the doctor his own point of view on the reasons for his illness and the nature of his experiences. The doctor, for his part, aims at enforcing his authority as a doctor, endeavors to wrest confessions from the patient and to compel him to take the "correct" point of view on his illness and its symptoms. Intertwining with all this are other factors: Between doctor and patient there may be differences in sex, in age, in social standing, and, moreover, there is the difference of their professions. All these factors complicate their relationship and the struggle between them.

And it is in the midst of this complex and very special social atmosphere that the verbal utterances are made—the patient's narratives and his statements in conversation with the doctor—utterances that Freud places squarely at the basis of his theory. Can we acknowledge these utterances as the expression of the patient's individual psyche?

Not a single instance of verbal utterance can be reckoned exclusively to its utterer's account. Every utterance is *the product of the interaction between speakers* and the product of the broader context of the whole complex *social situation* in which the utterance emerges. Elsewhere[1] we have attempted to show that any product of the activity of human discourse—from the simplest utterance in everyday life to elaborate works of literary art—derives shape and meaning in all its most essential aspects not from the subjective experiences of the speaker but from the social situation in which the utterance appears. Language and its forms are the products of prolonged social intercourse among members of a given speech community. An utterance finds language basically already prepared for use. It is the material for the utterance and it sets constraints on the utterance's possibilities. What is characteristic for a given utterance specifically—its selection of particular words, its particular kind of sentence structure, its particular kind of intonation—all this is the expression of the interrelationship between the speakers and of the whole complex set of social circumstances under which the exchange of words takes place. Those "psychical experiences" of the speaker, the expression of which we are inclined to see in his utterance, are, however, only in fact a one-sided, simplified, and scientifically unverifiable interpretation of a more complex social phenomenon. What we have here is a special kind of "projection," a means whereby we project into the "individual soul" a complex set of social interrelationships. Discourse is like a "scenario" of the immediate act of communication in the process of which it is engendered, and this act of communication is, in turn, a factor of the wider field of communication of the community to which the speaker belongs. In order to understand this "scenario," it is essential to reconstruct all those complex social interrelations of which the given utterance is the ideological refraction.

Nothing changes at all if, instead of outward speech, we are dealing with inner speech. Inner speech, too, assumes a listener and is oriented in its construction toward that listener. Inner speech is the same kind of product and expression of social intercourse as is outward speech.

All those verbal utterances of the patient (his verbal reactions), on which Freud's psychological system depends, are also just such *scenarios*, scenarios, first and foremost of the immediate, small social event in which they were engendered—the *psychoanalytical session*. Therein that complex struggle between doctor and patient, of which we spoke above, finds expression. What is reflected in these utterances is not the dynamics of the individual psyche but the *social dynamics* of the interrelations between doctor and patient. Here is the

[1]See our article, "Slovo v žizni i slovo v poèzii" [Discourse in Life and Discourse in Art], *Zvezda* 6 (1926). [An English translation of this article appears on pp. 93–116 of this book. *Translator*]

source for the dramatism that marks the Freudian construct. It is also the source for that personification of psychical forces which we have already mentioned. Here, indeed, people, not natural forces, are in conflict.

The psychical "mechanisms" readily disclose their social derivation to us. The "unconscious" stands in opposition not to the individual conscious of the patient but, primarily, to the doctor, his requirements and his views. "Resistance" is likewise primarily resistance to the doctor, to the listener, to the *other* person generally.

Freud's system *projects* the entire dynamics of the interrelationship between two people into the individual psyche. This sort of projection comes as no surprise; it is, as we have already said, a common phenomenon in subjective psychology. Psychical experiences, in the majority of instances, merely duplicate the world of external objects and social relations. Subjective idealism was only being consistent when it asserted that the whole world is nothing but the experience of the subject. When contemporary psychology attempts to draw a borderline between experience and things, it is compelled ultimately to come to the paradoxical conclusion that there is no such borderline, that everything depends on the point of view. One and the same thing, depending on the connection and the context in which we perceive it, is now a psychical experience (my sensation, my presentation), now a physical body or social phenomenon. The most radical conclusions in this regard were reached by one of the most eminent representatives of subjective psychology, William James. In his famous article "Does 'Consciousness' Exist?" James comes to the conclusion that *things and thoughts are made of the same material, that consciousness does not introduce a new reality into the world*—it is only *another point of view* on those very same things and phenomena.

Thus, Freudian psychical dynamics and its mechanisms are only a projection into the individual psyche of social interrelationships. It makes for a complex, dramatically charged image, and Freud employs it in his effort to interpret various aspects of human behavior, remaining within the confines of only one sector of that behavior—*the verbal reactions of human beings.*

We must turn attention to still another aspect of the Freudian system. The content of the unconscious, that is, various repressed complexes (including above all the Oedipus complex), is relegated by Freud to a person's past, to his early years of childhood. But the entire doctrine on these early, preconscious stages of human development is built on the basis of evidence supplied by adults. Those few attempts the Freudians did make to analyze the behavior of children *directly*[2] did not have, and could not have had, any substantive importance for

---

[2] The most important work of Freud's devoted to analysis of childhood nervous disorders is: "Geschichte der Fobie eines 5-jährigen Knaben," in *Kleine Schriften zur Neurosenlehre*, Part 3.

the working out of the Freudian construct. That construct took shape independently of such attempts and even before they were made, and the analyses themselves already presupposed and entirely depended on it. Thus, the whole construct of infantile complexes was obtained by *retrospective means*; it is based on the interpretation of the remembrances of adults and of those compromise formations with the aid of which those remembrances could be reached (let us recall here the dream analysis quoted above that delved down to the hidden remembrances of the Oedipus complex).

Can such a retrospective method of reconstructing experiences from early childhood (a complex, after all, is a set of experiences)—can such a method be considered scientifically sound?

We believe that nothing real, nothing objective can possibly be arrived at that way. What we are dealing with here is, in fact, a very widespread and typical phenomenon: *the interpretation of the past from the point of view of the present.* Anything like objective remembrance of our past inner experiences is, of course, entirely out of the question. We see in the past only what is important for the present, important for the instant in which we remember our past. We transfer from the present to the preconscious past of the child above all that ideological-evaluative complexion which is characteristic of the present only. All those evaluations, points of view, associations that have coalesced in the conscious period of our life with such concepts as "love," "sexual attraction," "mother," endowing these concepts with their own complexion and making them meaningful for us, are what we then transfer to the interpretation of the facts of childhood and thereby create out of those facts of childhood coherent and meaningful events like those of adult life.

"Sexual attraction to the mother," "the father rival," "hostility toward the father," "wish for the father's death"—if we subtract from all these "events" that ideational significance, that evaluative tone, that full measure of ideological weight which accrue to them only in the context of our conscious "adult" present, what would they have left?

They would, in any case, retain nothing that would give us the serious right to speak about an Oedipus complex, that is, about a repetition of the scheme of the Oedipus tragedy in a child's life. Precisely that aspect which gives the tragedy its profound and harrowing meaning, which horrifies and astounds the audience— that aspect would certainly be missing.

What would remain, then? A number of piecemeal objective observations that can be made about the behavior of a child: the early excitability of the sexual organs (e.g., infant erection) and of other erogenous zones, the difficulty of weaning a child away from his constant closeness to his mother's body (particularly, of course, the breast), and so on. There is obviously no need to contest a set of facts of this sort—they are commonly accepted facts. But from a series of such facts to the grandiose and startling construct of the Oedipus complex there is a vast abyss. Once you give up projecting into the past the points of view, evaluations, and interpretations that belong to the present, then you have no cause to speak about any such thing as an Oedipus complex, no matter how great the quantity of objective facts cited in proof.

The Freudians often challenge their critics by saying: If you want to refute the psychoanalytical theory, then you must first refute the facts on which it rests.

That sort of statement is already wrong in its assumptions. It distorts the actual state of affairs. Freudianism is not at all a series of facts and not at all that minimum of a working hypothesis necessary for preliminary organization and classification of those facts. Freudianism is a grandiose construct based on an extremely daring and original interpretation of facts, a construct that would not cease to astound us as something strange and paradoxical even if all the external facts advanced to prove it were accepted.

Facts are tested and verified or rejected by repeated observations or control experiments. But they can have no reflection on one's critical attitude toward the bases of the theoretical construct. Let us take Rank's thoroughly outlandish construct, the "trauma of birth." In order to declare this theory, at the very least, improbable, do we really need to refute the fact that the organism experiences a physiological shock at the moment the child is born into the world (the action of expulsion, the spasm of the first breath of air into the lungs, the effect of the atmosphere and so on)? The fact itself is correct (although it has still not been subjected to detailed scientific investigation) and is a piece of common knowledge. And all the same, when you read Rank's book you cannot help but wonder: Does he mean all this "seriously" or is he doing it "on purpose"?

Exactly the same thing has to be said about the relation of the facts of infantile sexuality to the construct of the Oedipus complex. The facts cannot confirm the Oedipus complex because the facts belong to a different level, a different set of dimensions, than it does. The facts pertain to external, objective apprehension; the construct, to the sphere of inner experiences in a child's psyche. Moreover, in order to have any right at all to speak of infantile sexuality, the word "sexuality" has to be understood to mean only a set of strictly defined physiological manifestations. If, on the contrary, we have in mind experiences pertaining to internal apprehension, experiences that are associated with those physiological manifestations but are permeated with value judgements and points of view, then we are making an arbitrary construct; instead of the physiological fact of sexuality, we take its ideological formulation. *The construct of the Oedipus complex is just such a purely ideological formulation projected into the psyche of a child.* The Oedipus complex is not at all the unadulterated expression of objective physiological facts.

The same must also be said about the other factors in the content of the unconscious. Everything involved here is a projection into the past of ideological interpretations of behavior that are characteristic for the present only. Freud nowhere steps beyond the confines of a subjective construct.

What, then, remains of the "dynamics" of the psyche once we subtract the constructs that are untenable for us?—Conflicts within the verbalized behavior of human beings. A struggle of motives, but not a struggle of natural forces.

Behind this struggle, as behind any ideological struggle of whatever scale, certain objective, material processes are covertly present. But Freudianism has not disclosed these processes. Indeed, to discover them would require going beyond the limits of subjective psychology, going beyond the limits of every-thing that a person himself could say about himself on the basis of his own inner apprehension, no matter how broadly that apprehension be understood.

Certain of these objective facts of behavior are physiological (ultimately, physiochemical) in character. Such facts can be studied by the methods that form the basis of the reflex doctrine of Academician Pavlov and his school or by the methods that have been so brilliantly and soundly argued by the late Jacques Loeb in his renowned theory of tropisms[3] or by other variants of the basically unitary physiological method. But when it comes to an explanation of human behavior all this supplies us very little. In particular, those conflicts of verbalized behavior, with which Freudianism confronts us, need, if they are to be properly understood, a rigorous and thoroughgoing account of socioeconomic factors. Only with the help of the flexible methods of dialectical materialism have we the possibility of illuminating those conflicts.

What we call the "human psyche" and "consciousness" reflects the dialectics of history to a much greater degree than the dialectics of nature. The nature that is present in them is nature already in economic and social refraction.

The content of the human psyche—a content consisting of thoughts, feelings, desires—is given in a formulation made by consciousness and, consequently, in the formulation of human verbal discourse. Verbal discourse, not in its narrow linguistic sense, but in its broad and concrete sociological sense—*that* is the *objective milieu* in which the content of the psyche is presented. It is here that motives of behavior, arguments, goals, evaluations are composed and given external expression. It is here, too, that arise the conflicts among them.

It is not within the purposes of a critique such as ours to introduce a positive program on the motives and conflicts of verbalized behavior. We can only point out the direction in which an objective understanding and study of these phenomena could be made possible.

---

[3] See Jacques Loeb, *Forced Movements, Tropisms, and Animal Conduct* (Philadelphia and London, 1918) and [original English title unknown. *Translator*] "Značenie tropizmov dlja psixologii" [The Significance of Tropisms for Psychology], *Novye idei v filosofii*, No. 8.

CHAPTER 9

The Content of Consciousness
as Ideology

The sociological character of verbal reactions. Methods for studying the content of consciousness. The concept of "behavioral ideology." The various levels of "behavioral ideology." The sexual. Conclusions.

We know that Freudianism began from a position of distrust of the conscious and fundamental criticism of motives such as those a person is likely, in all honesty and sincerity, to use as explanations for and commentary on his behavior (let us recall Bernheim's experiment). Consciousness is in fact *that commentary* which every adult human being brings to bear on every instance of his behavior. According to Freud, this commentary is invalid; any psychology that takes such commentary as its basis is likewise invalid.

Wherever Freud criticizes the psychology of consciousness, we can join in full accord with him. A person's conscious motivation of his actions is certainly in no instance to be taken as a scientific explanation of his behavior. But we go further than that. Neither do the motives of the unconscious explain his behavior in the least, for, as we have seen, the Freudian unconscious does not fundamentally differ from consciousness; it is only another form of consciousness, only an ideologically different expression of it.

The motives of the unconscious that are disclosed at psychoanalytical sessions with the aid of "free association" are just such *verbal reactions* on the patient's part as are all other, ordinary motives of consciousness. They differ from the latter not in kind of "being," that is, not ontologically, but only in terms of content, that is, *ideologically.* In this sense Freud's unconscious can be called the "unofficial conscious" in distinction from the ordinary "official conscious."

From the objective point of view, both sets of motives, those of the unofficial as well as of the official conscious, are given completely alike in inner and in outward speech and both alike are not a cause of behavior but a component, an integral part of it. For objective psychology, every human motive belongs to human behavior as a part of it and not a cause of it. Human behavior may be said to break down into motor reactions ("acts" in the narrow sense of the word) and reactions of *inner and outward speech* (verbal reactions) that accompany motor reactions. Both these components of the whole of human behavior are objective and material in nature and require for their explanation factors that are likewise objective and material with respect both to the human organism itself and to the surrounding natural and social environment.

The verbal component of behavior is determined in all the fundamentals and essentials of its content by objective-social factors.

The social environment is what has given a person words and what has joined words with specific meanings and value judgements; the same environment continues ceaselessly to determine and control a person's verbal reactions throughout his entire life.

Therefore, nothing verbal in human behavior (inner and outward speech equally) can under any circumstances be reckoned to the account of the individual subject in isolation; the verbal is not his property but the property of his *social group* (his social milieu).

In the preceding chapter we pointed out that every concrete utterance always reflects the *immediate* small social event—the event of communication, of exchange of words between persons—out of which it directly arose. We saw that Freud's "dynamics" reflected the psychoanalytical session with its struggle and peripeteia—that social event out of which the patient's verbal utterances were engendered. In the present chapter what interests us is not the immediate context of utterance but the broader, more enduring and steadfast social connections out of whose dynamics are generated all elements of the form and content of our inner and outward speech, the whole repertoire of value judgements, points of view, approaches, and so on with the help of which we illuminate for ourselves and for others our actions, desires, feelings, and sensations.

This content of our consciousness and of our psyche in its entirety and, likewise, the separate and individual utterances with the help of which that content and that psyche manifest themselves outwardly are in every respect determined by socioeconomic factors.

We shall never reach the real, substantive roots of any given single utterance if we look for them within the confines of the single, individual organism, even when that utterance concerns what appears to be the most private and most intimate side of a person's life. Any motivation of one's behavior, any instance of self-awareness (for self-awareness is always verbal, always a matter of finding some specifically suitable verbal complex) is an act of gauging oneself against some social norm, social evaluation—is, so to speak, the socialization of oneself and one's behavior. In becoming aware of myself, I attempt to look at myself, as it were, through the eyes of another person, another representative of my social group, my class. Thus, *self-consciousness*, in the final analysis, always leads us to *class consciousness*, the reflection and specification of which it is in all its fundamental and essential respects. Here we have the *objective roots* of even the most personal and intimate reactions.

How do we reach those roots?

With the help of those objective-sociological methods that Marxism has worked out for the analysis of various ideological systems—law, morality, science, world outlook, art, religion.

In bourgeois philosophy the contention has long held sway, and is even now quite widespread, that a work of cultural creativity can be considered fully explained if the analyst succeeds in reducing it to the specific individual states of mind and psychical experiences of the person who created it. This contention, as we have seen, is upheld by the Freudians, as well. But in actual fact there is no fundamental dividing line between the content of the individual psyche and formulated ideology. In any case, the content of the individual psyche is not the least bit easier to understand or clearer than the content of cultural creativity and, therefore, cannot serve as explication for it. An experience of which an individual is conscious is already ideological and, therefore, from a scientific point of view, can in no way be a primary and irreducible datum; rather, it is an entity that has already undergone ideological processing of some specific kind. The haziest content of consciousness of the primitive savage and the most sophisticated cultural monument are only extreme links in the single chain of ideological creativity. Between them exists a whole unbroken series of degrees and transitions.

The more clarified a thought of mine becomes, the closer it will approach the formulated products of scientific creativity. What is more, my thought will be able to achieve final clarity only when I find exact verbal formulation for it and bring it into contact with scientific postulations that have a bearing on the same topic—in other words, my thought will not achieve final clarity until I transform it into an authoritative scientific product. Similarly, a feeling cannot achieve culmination and definitiveness without finding its external expression, without nurturing itself on words, rhythm, color, that is, without being forged into a work of art.

The route leading from the content of the individual psyche to the content of culture is a long and hard one, but it is a single route, and throughout its entire extent at every stage it is determined by one and the same socioeconomic governance.

At all stages of this route the human consciousness operates through words— that medium which is the most sensitive and at the same time the most complicated refraction of the socioeconomic governance. For the study of verbal reactions in their most primitive, pragmatic form, the same methods must be used as Marxism has worked out for the study of complex ideological constructs, since the laws of the refraction of objective necessity in verbal discourse are one and the same in both instances.

Any human verbal utterance is an ideological construct in the small. The motivation of one's behavior is juridical and moral creativity on a small scale; an exclamation of joy or grief is a primitive lyric composition; pragmatic considerations of the causes and consequences of happenings are germinal forms of scientific and philosophical cognition, and so on and so forth. The stable, formulated ideological systems of the sciences, the arts, jurisprudence, and the like have sprung and crystallized from that seething ideological element whose broad waves of inner and outward speech engulf our every act and our every perception. Of course, an ideology, once it has achieved formulation, exerts, in turn, a reverse influence on our verbal reactions.

Let us call that inner and outward speech that permeates our behavior in all its aspects "behavioral ideology." This behavioral ideology is in certain respects more sensitive, more responsive, more excitable and livelier than an ideology that has undergone formulation and become "official." In the depths of behavioral ideology accumulate those contradictions which, once having reached a certain threshold, ultimately burst asunder the system of the official ideology. But, on the whole, we may say that behavioral ideology relates just as much to the socioeconomic basis and is subject to the same laws of development as ideological superstructures in the proper sense of the term. Therefore, the methods for its study should be, as already stated, basically the same methods, only somewhat differentiated and modified in accordance with the special nature of the material.

Let us now return to those "psychical" conflicts upon which psychoanalysis is based and which psychoanalysis attempts to explain in terms of a struggle between the conscious and the unconscious. From an objective point of view, all these conflicts are played out in the element of inner and outward speech (in addition, of course, to their purely physiological aspect), that is to say, they are played out in the element of behavioral ideology. They are not "psychical" but ideological conflicts and, therefore, they cannot be understood within the narrow confines of the individual organism and the individual psyche. They not only go beyond the conscious, as Freud believes, they also go beyond the individual as a whole.

Dream, myth, joke, witticism, and all the verbal components of the pathological formations reflect the struggle of various ideological tendencies and trends that take shape within *behavioral ideology*.

Those areas of behavioral ideology that correspond to Freud's official, "censored" conscious express the most steadfast and the governing factors of class consciousness. They lie close to the formulated, fully fledged ideology of the class in question, its law, its morality, its world outlook. On these levels of behavioral ideology, inner speech comes easily to order and freely turns into outward speech or, in any case, has no fear of becoming outward speech.

Other levels, corresponding to Freud's unconscious, lie at a great distance from the stable system of the ruling ideology. They bespeak the disintegration of the unity and integrity of the system, the vulnerability of the usual ideological motivations. Of course, instances of the accumulation of such inner motives— ones that erode the unity of behavioral ideology—can bear an incidental character and testify merely to the *assumption of a social déclassé status* on the part of separate individuals, but more often they testify to the emergent disintegration if not of the class as a whole then of certain of its groups. *In a healthy community and in a socially healthy personality, behavioral ideology, founded on the socioeconomic basis, is strong and sound*—here, there is no discrepancy between the official and the unofficial conscious.

The content and composition of the unofficial levels of behavioral ideology (in Freudian terms, the content and composition of the unconscious) are conditioned by historical time and class to the same degree as are its levels "under censorship" and its systems of formulated ideology (morality, law, world outlook). For example, the homosexual inclinations of an ancient Hellene of the ruling class produced absolutely no conflicts in his behavioral ideology; they freely emerged into outward speech and even found formulated ideological expression (e.g., Plato's *Symposium*).

All those conflicts with which psychoanalysis deals are characteristic in the highest degree for the European petite bourgeoisie of modern times. Freud's "censorship" very distinctly reflects the behavioral-ideological point of view of a petit bourgeois, and for that reason a somewhat comical effect is produced when Freudians transfer that point of view to the psyche of an ancient Greek or a medieval peasant. The monstrous overestimation on Freudianism's part of the sexual factor is also exceedingly revealing against the background of the present disintegration of the bourgeois family.

The wider and deeper the breach between the official and the unofficial conscious, the more difficult it becomes for motives of inner speech to turn into outward speech (oral or written or printed, in a circumscribed or broad social milieu) wherein they might acquire formulation, clarity, and rigor. Motives under these conditions begin to fail, to lose their verbal countenance, and little by little really do turn into a "foreign body" in the psyche. Whole sets of organic manifestations come, in this way, to be excluded from the zone of verbalized behavior and may become *asocial*. Thereby the sphere of the "animalian" in man enlarges.

Of course, not every area of human behavior is subject to so complete a divorce from verbal ideological formulation. After all, neither is it true that every motive in contradiction with the official ideology must degenerate into indistinct inner speech and then die out—it might well engage in a struggle with that official ideology. If such a motive *is founded on the economic being of the whole group*, if it is not merely the motive of a déclassé loner, then it has a chance for a future and perhaps even a victorious future. There is no reason why such a motive should become asocial and lose contact with communication. Only, at first a motive of this sort will develop within a small social milieu and will depart into the underground—not the psychological underground of repressed complexes, but the salutary political underground. That is exactly how a *revolutionary ideology* in all spheres of culture comes about.

There is one other extremely important area of human behavior in which verbal connections are put in order with great difficulty and which, therefore, is especially liable to fall out of social context, lose its ideological formulatedness, and degenerate into an aboriginal, animalian state. This is the area of *the sexual*. The disintegration of an official ideology is reflected first and foremost in this area of human behavior. It becomes the center for the accumulation of asocial and antisocial forces.

This area of human private life is preeminently the one most easily made the base for social deviations. The sexual "pair," as a sort of *social minimum*, is most easily isolated and transformed into a microcosm without the need for anything or anybody else.

All periods of social decline and disintegration are characterized by *overestimation of the sexual* in life and in ideology, and what is more, of the sexual in an extreme unidimensional conception; its *asocial* aspect, taken in isolation, is advanced to the forefront. The sexual aims at becoming a surrogate for the social. All human beings are divided above all into males and females. All the remaining subdivisions are held to be inessential. Only those social relations that can be sexualized are meaningful and valuable. Everything else becomes null and void.

The present day success of Freudianism throughout Europe bespeaks the complete disintegration of the *official ideological system*. A "behavioral ideology" has supervened that is turned in upon itself, disjointed, unformulated. Each aspect of life, each happening and object, goes out of kilter with a smoothly operating and universally respected context of *class and social values*. Each thing, as it were, turns its sexual, not its social, side to the human gaze. Behind every word in a poetic or philosophical text glares some stark sexual symbol. All other aspects of words, and especially the social-historical values inherent in them, cease to be heard by a modern European bourgeois—they have become merely overtones to the basic note of sexuality.

An extremely indicative and immensely interesting feature of Freudianism is its *wholesale sexualization of the family* and all family relationships in toto (the Oedipus complex). The family, that castle and keep of capitalism, evidently has become a thing economically and socially little understood and little taken to heart; and that is what has brought on its wholesale sexualization, as if thereby it were made newly meaningful or "made strange" as our formalists would say.[1] The Oedipus complex is indeed a magnificent way of making the family unit "strange." The father is not the entrepreneur, and the son is not his heir—the father is only the mother's lover, and his son is his rival!

Precisely this novel and piquant "meaningfulness," imparted to all those aspects of life that have lost their meaning, is what has attracted so broad a public to Freudianism. The obviousness and certitude of sexual drives contrast here with the ambiguity and uncertainty of all other social ideological values. Sexuality is declared the supreme criterion of *reality*, of essentiality. And the more déclassé a person is, the more keenly he senses his "naked naturalness," his "elementalness."

Freudianism—the psychology of the déclassés—is becoming the acknowledged ideological persuasion of the widest strata of the European bourgeoisie. Here is a fact profoundly symptomatic and indicative for anybody who wishes to grasp the spirit of Europe today.

The basic aspiration of the philosophy of our time is *to create a world beyond the social and the historical*. The "cosmism" of Steiner's anthroposophy, the "biologism" of Bergson, and, finally, the "psychobiologism" and "sexualism" of Freud that we have examined here—all these three trends, sharing the entire bourgeois world among them, have, each in its own way, served the aspiration of the latest philosophy. They have endowed with their own features the physiognomy of the modern *Kulturmensch*—the Steinerian, the Bergsonian, the Freudian—and they have raised the *three altars* of his belief and veneration— *Magic, Instinct* and *Sex*. Where the creative paths of history are closed, there remain only the blind alleys of the individual "livings out" of a life bereft of meaning.

---

[1] "Making strange" (*ostranenie*) is a verbal device whereby an ordinary and familiar thing is made to appear new and strange. [On the Russian formalist notion of *ostranenie*, see V. Erlich, *Russian Formalism (History-Doctrine)* (The Hague, 1955) pp. 150-151; on the formalists and Vološinov's position in their regard, see pp. 96–97 of this book and Appendix 2 in V. N. Vološinov, *Marxism and the Philosophy of Language* (New York and London; Seminar Press 1973), especially pp. 175-180. *Translator*]

Discourse in Life and Discourse in Art
(Concerning Sociological Poetics)

V. N. Vološinov

I

In the study of literature, the sociological method has been applied almost exclusively for treating historical questions while remaining virtually untouched with regard to the problems of so-called *theoretical poetics*—that whole area of issues involving artistic form and its various factors, style, and so forth.

A fallacious view, but one adhered to even by certain Marxists, has it that the sociological method becomes legitimate only at that point where poetic form acquires added complexity through the ideological factor (the content) and begins to develop historically in conditions of external social reality. Form in and of itself, according to this view, possesses its own special, not sociological, but specifically artistic nature and system of governance.

Such a view fundamentally contradicts the very bases of the Marxist method— its monism and its historicity. The consequence of this and similar views is that form and content, theory and history are rent asunder.

But we cannot dismiss these fallacious views without further, more detailed inquiry; they are too characteristic for the whole of the modern study of the arts.

The most patent and consistent development of the point of view in question appeared recently in a work by Professor P. N. Sakulin.[1] Sakulin distinguishes two dimensions in literature and its history: the immanent and the causal. The immanent "artistic core" of literature possesses special structure and governance peculiar to itself alone; so endowed, it is capable of autonomous evolutionary

---

[1] P. N. Sakulin, *Sociologičeskij metod v literaturovedenii* [The Sociological Method in the Study of Literature] (1925).

development "by nature." But in the process of this development, literature becomes subject to the "causal" influence of the extraartistic social milieu. With the "immanent core" of literature, its structure and autonomous evolution, the sociologist can have nothing to do—those topics fall within the exclusive competence of theoretical and historical poetics and their special methods.[2] The sociological method can successfully study only the causal interaction between literature and its surrounding extraartistic social milieu. Moreover, immanent (nonsociological) analysis of the essence of literature, including its intrinsic, autonomous governance, must precede sociological analysis.[3]

Of course, no Marxist sociologist could agree with such an assertion. Nevertheless, it has to be admitted that sociology, up to the present moment, has dealt almost exclusively with concrete issues in history of literature and has not made a single serious attempt to utilize its methods in the study of the so-called "immanent" structure of a work of art. That structure has, in plain fact, been relegated to the province of aesthetic or psychological or other methods that have nothing in common with sociology.

To verify this fact we need only examine any modern work on poetics or even on the theory of art study in general. We will not find a trace of any application of sociological categories. Art is treated as if it were nonsociological "by nature," just exactly as is the physical or chemical structure of a body. Most West European and Russian scholars of the arts make precisely this claim regarding literature and art as a whole, and on this basis persistently defend the study of art as a special discipline against sociological approaches of any kind.

They motivate this claim of theirs in approximately the following way. Every item that becomes the object of supply and demand, that is, that becomes a commodity, is subject, as concerns its value and its circulation within human society, to the governing socioeconomic laws. Let us suppose that we know those laws very well; still, despite that fact, we shall understand exactly nothing

---

[2] "Elements of poetic form (sound, word, image, rhythm, composition, genre), poetic thematics, artistic style in its totality—all these things are studied, as preliminary matters, with the help of methods that have been worked out by theoretical poetics, grounded in psychology, aesthetics, and linguistics, and that are now practiced in particular by the so-called formal method." *Ibid.*, p. 27.

[3] "Viewing literature as a social phenomenon, we inevitably arrive at the question of its causal conditioning. For us this is a matter of sociological causality. Only at the present time has the historian of literature received the right to assume the position of a sociologist and to pose 'why' questions so as to include literary facts within the general process of the social life of some particular period and so as to, thereupon, define the place of literature in the whole movement of history. It is at this point that the sociological method, as applied to history of literature, becomes a historical-sociological method.

In the first, immanent stage, a work was conceived of as an artistic value and not in its social and historical meaning." *Ibid.*, pp. 27, 28.

about the physical and chemical structure of the item in question. On the contrary, the study of commodities is itself in need of preliminary physical and chemical analysis of the given commodity. And the only persons competent to perform such analyses are physicists and chemists with the help of the specific methods of their fields. In the opinion of these art scholars, art stands in an analogous position. Art, too, once it becomes a social factor and becomes subject to the influence of other, likewise social, factors, takes its place, of course, within the overall system of sociological governance—but from that governance we shall never be able to derive art's *aesthetic essence*, just as we cannot derive the chemical formula for this or that commodity from the governing economic laws of commodity circulation. What art study and theoretical poetics are supposed to do is to seek such a formula for a work of art—one that is *specific* to art and independent of sociology.

This conception of the essence of art is, as we have said, fundamentally in contradiction with the bases of Marxism. To be sure, you will never find a chemical formula by the sociological method, but a scientific "formula" for any domain of *ideology* can be found, and can only be found, by the methods of sociology. All the other—"immanent"—methods are heavily involved in subjectivism and have been unable, to the present day, to break free of the fruitless controversy of opinions and points of view and, therefore, are least of all capable of finding anything even remotely resembling the rigorous and exact formulas of chemistry. Neither, of course, can the Marxist method claim to provide such a "formula"; the rigor and exactness of the natural sciences are impossible within the domain of ideological study due to the very nature of what it studies. But the closest approximation to genuine scientificness in the study of ideological creativity has become possible for the first time thanks to the sociological method in its Marxist conception. Physical and chemical bodies or substances exist outside human society as well as within it, but all products of ideological creativity arise in and for human society. Social definitions are not applicable from outside, as is the case with bodies and substances in nature—*ideological formations are intrinsically, immanently sociological.* No one is likely to dispute that point with respect to political and juridical forms—what possible nonsociological, immanent property could be found in them? The most subtle formal nuances of a law or of a political system are all equally amenable to the sociological method and only to it. But exactly the same thing is true for other ideological forms. They are all *sociological through and through*, even though their structure, mutable and complex as it is, lends itself to exact analysis only with enormous difficulty.

Art, too, is just as immanently social; the extraartistic social milieu, affecting art from outside, finds direct, intrinsic response within it. This is not a case of one foreign element affecting another but of one social formation affecting another social formation. The *aesthetic*, just as the juridical or the cognitive, is *only a variety of the social*. Theory of art, consequently, can only be a *sociology of art*.[4] No "immanent" tasks are left in its province.

II

If sociological analysis is to be properly and productively applied to the theory of art (poetics in particular), then two fallacious views that severely narrow the scope of art by operating exclusively with certain isolated factors must be rejected.

The first view can be defined as the *fetishization of the artistic work artifact*. This fetishism is the prevailing attitude in the study of art at the present time. The field of investigation is restricted to the work of art itself, which is analyzed in such a way as if everything in art were exhausted by it alone. The creator of the work and the work's contemplators remain outside the field of investigation.

The second point of view, conversely, restricts itself to the study of the psyche of the creator or of the contemplator (more often than not, it simply equates the two). For it, all art is exhausted by the experiences of the person doing the contemplating or doing the creating.

Thus, for the one point of view the object of study is only the structure of the work artifact, while for the other it is only the individual psyche of the creator or contemplator.

The first point of view advances the material to the forefront of aesthetic investigation. Form, understood very narrowly as the form of the material—that which organizes it into a single unified and complete artifact—becomes the main and very nearly exclusive object of study.

A variety of the first point of view is the so-called formal method. For the formal method, a poetic work is verbal material organized by form in some particular way. Moreover, it takes *the verbal* not as a sociological phenomenon but from an abstract linguistic point of view. That it should adopt just such a point of view is quite understandable. Verbal discourse, taken in the broader sense as a phenomenon of cultural communication, ceases to be something self-contained and can no longer be understood independently of the social situation that engenders it.

The first point of view cannot be consistently followed out to the end. The problem is that if one remains within the confines of the artifact aspect of art, there is no way of indicating even such things as the boundaries of the material or which of its features have artistic significance. The material in and of itself

---

[4] We make a distinction between theory and history of art only as a matter of a technical division of labor. There cannot be any methodological breach between them. Historical categories are of course applicable in absolutely all the fields of the humanities, whether they be historical or theoretical ones.

directly merges with the extraartistic milieu surrounding it and has an infinite number of aspects and definitions—in terms of mathematics, physics, chemistry, and so forth as well as of linguistics. However far we go in analyzing all the properties of the material and all the possible combinations of those properties, we shall never be able to find their aesthetic significance unless we slip in the contraband of another point of view that does not belong within the framework of analysis of the material. Similarly, however far we go in analyzing the chemical structure of a body or substance, we shall never understand its value and significance as a commodity unless we draw economics into the picture.

The attempt of the second view to find the aesthetic in the individual psyche of the creator or contemplator is equally vain. To continue our economic analogy, we might say that such a thing is similar to the attempt to analyze the individual psyche of a proletarian in order thereby to disclose the objective production relations that determine his position in society.

In the final analysis, both points of view are guilty of the same fault: *They attempt to discover the whole in the part,* that is, they take the structure of a part, abstractly divorced from the whole, and claim it as the structure of the whole. Meanwhile, "the artistic" in its total integrity is not located in the artifact and not located in the separately considered psyches of creator and contemplator; it encompasses all three of these factors. It is a *special form of interrelationship between creator and contemplator fixed in a work of art.*

This *artistic communication* stems from the basis common to it and other social forms, but, at the same time, it retains, as do all other forms, its own uniqueness; it is a special type of communication, possessing a form of its own peculiar to itself. *To understand this special form of social communication realized and fixed in the material of a work of art—that precisely is the task of sociological poetics.*

A work of art, viewed outside this communication and independently of it, is simply a physical artifact or an exercise in linguistics. It becomes art only in the process of the interaction between creator and contemplator, as the essential factor in this interaction. Everything in the material of a work of art that cannot be drawn into the communication between creator and contemplator, that cannot become the "medium," the means of their communication, cannot be the recipient of artistic value, either.

Those methods that ignore the social essence of art and attempt to find its nature and distinguishing features only in the organization of the work artifact are in actuality obliged to project the social interrelationship of creator and contemplator into various aspects of the material and into various devices for structuring the material. In exactly the same way, psychological aesthetics projects the same social relations into the individual psyche of the perceiver. This projection distorts the integrity of these interrelationships and gives a false picture of both the material and the psyche.

Aesthetic communication, fixed in a work of art, is, as we have already said, entirely unique and irreducible to other types of ideological communication such as the political, the juridical, the moral, and so on. If political communication establishes corresponding institutions and, at the same time, juridical forms, aesthetic communication organizes only a work of art. If the latter rejects this task and begins to aim at creating even the most transitory of political organizations or any other ideological form, then by that very fact it ceases to be aesthetic communication and relinquishes its unique character. *What characterizes aesthetic communication is the fact that it is wholly absorbed in the creation of a work of art, and in its continuous re-creations in the co-creation of contemplators, and does not require any other kind of objectification.* But, needless to say, this unique form of communication does not exist *in isolation*; it participates in the unitary flow of social life, it reflects the common economic basis, and it engages in interaction and exchange with other forms of communication.

The purpose of the present study is to try to reach an understanding of the poetic utterance as a form of this special, verbally implemented aesthetic communication. But in order to do so, we must first analyze in detail certain aspects of verbal utterances outside the realm of art—utterances in the *speech of everyday life and behavior*, for in such speech are already embedded the bases, the potentialities of artistic form. Moreover, the social essence of verbal discourse stands out here in sharper relief and the connection between an utterance and the surrounding social milieu lends itself more easily to analysis.

III

In life, verbal discourse is clearly not self-sufficient. It arises out of an extraverbal pragmatic situation and maintains the closest possible connection with that situation. Moreover, such discourse is directly informed by life itself and cannot be divorced from life without losing its import.

The kind of characterizations and evaluations of pragmatic, behavioral utterances we are likely to make are such things as: "that's a lie," "that's the truth," "that's a daring thing to say," "you can't say that," and so on and so forth.

All these and similar evaluations, whatever the criteria that govern them (ethical, cognitive, political, or other), take in a good deal more than what is enclosed within the strictly verbal (linguistic) factors of the utterance. *Together with the verbal factors, they also take in the extraverbal situation of the utterance*. These judgements and evaluations refer to a certain whole wherein the verbal discourse directly engages an event in life and merges with that event, forming an indissoluble unity. The verbal discourse itself, taken in isolation as a purely linguistic phenomenon, cannot, of course, be true or false, daring or diffident.

How does verbal discourse in life relate to the extraverbal situation that has engendered it? Let us analyze this matter, using an intentionally simplified example for the purpose.

Two people are sitting in a room. They are both silent. Then one of them says, "Well!" The other does not respond.

For us, as outsiders, this entire "conversation" is utterly incomprehensible. Taken in isolation, the utterance "Well!" is empty and unintelligible. Nevertheless, this peculiar colloquy of two persons, consisting of only one—although, to be sure, one expressively intoned—word, does make perfect sense, is fully meaningful and complete.

In order to disclose the sense and meaning of this colloquy, we must analyze it. But what is it exactly that we can subject to analysis? Whatever pains we take with the purely verbal part of the utterance, however subtly we define the phonetic, morphological, and semantic factors of the word *well*, we shall still not come a single step closer to an understanding of the whole sense of the colloquy.

Let us suppose that the intonation with which this word was pronounced is known to us: indignation and reproach moderated by a certain amount of humor. This intonation somewhat fills in the semantic void of the adverb *well* but still does not reveal the meaning of the whole.

What is it we lack, then? We lack the "extraverbal context" that made the word *well* a meaningful locution for the listener. This *extraverbal context* of the utterance is comprised of three factors: (1) the *common spatial purview* of the interlocutors (the unity of the visible—in this case, the room, the window, and so on), (2) the interlocutors' *common knowledge and understanding of the situation*, and (3) their *common evaluation* of that situation.

At the time the colloquy took place, both interlocutors *looked up* at the window and *saw* that it had begun to snow; *both knew* that it was already May and that it was high time for spring to come; finally, *both* were *sick and tired* of the protracted winter—*they both were looking forward* to spring and *both were bitterly disappointed* by the late snowfall. On this "jointly seen" (snowflakes outside the window), "jointly known" (the time of year—May) and "unanimously evaluated" (winter wearied of, spring looked forward to)—on all this the utterance *directly depends*, all this is seized in its actual, living import—is its very sustenance. And yet all this remains without verbal specification or articulation. The snowflakes remain outside the window; the date, on the page of a calendar; the evaluation, in the psyche of the speaker; and nevertheless, all this is *assumed* in the word *well*.

Now that we have been let in on the "assumed," that is, now that we know the *shared spatial and ideational purview*, the whole sense of the utterance "Well!" is perfectly clear to us and we also understand its intonation.

How does the extraverbal purview relate to the verbal discourse, how does the said relate to the unsaid?

First of all, it is perfectly obvious that, in the given case, the discourse does not at all reflect the extraverbal situation in the way a mirror reflects an object. Rather, the discourse here *resolves the situation*, bringing it to an *evaluative conclusion*, as it were. Far more often, behavioral utterances actively continue and develop a situation, adumbrate a plan for future action, and organize that action. But for us it is another aspect of the behavioral utterance that is of special importance. Whatever kind it be, the behavioral utterance always joins the participants in the situation together as *co-participants* who know, understand, and evaluate the situation in like manner. *The utterance, consequently, depends on their real, material appurtenance to one and the same segment of being and gives this material commonness ideological expression and further ideological development.*

Thus, the extraverbal situation is far from being merely the external cause of an utterance—it does not operate on the utterance from outside, as if it were a mechanical force. Rather, *the situation enters into the utterance as an essential constitutive part of the structure of its import.* Consequently, a behavioral utterance as a meaningful whole is comprised of two parts: (1) the part realized or actualized in words and (2) the assumed part. On this basis, the behavioral utterance can be likened to the enthymeme.[5]

However, it is an enthymeme of a special order. The very term enthymeme (literally translated from the Greek, something located in the heart or mind) sounds a bit too psychological. One might be led to think of the situation as something in the mind of the speaker on the order of a subjective-psychical act (a thought, idea, feeling). But that is not the case. The individual and subjective are backgrounded here by *the social and objective*. What *I* know, see, want, love, and so on cannot be assumed. Only what all of us speakers know, see, love, recognize—only those points on which we are all united can become the assumed part of an utterance. Furthermore, this fundamentally social phenomenon is completely objective; it consists, above all, of *the material unity of world that enters the speakers' purview* (in our example, the room, the snow outside the window, and so on) and of *the unity of the real conditions of life* that generate a *community of value judgements*—the speakers' belonging to the same family, profession, class, or other social group, and their belonging to the same time period (the speakers are, after all, contemporaries). Assumed value judgements are, therefore, not individual emotions but regular and essential social acts. *Individual* emotions can come into play only as *overtones* accompanying the *basic tone of social evaluation*. "I" can realize itself verbally only on the basis of "we."

---

[5]The enthymeme is a form of syllogism one of whose premises is not expressed but assumed. For example: "Socrates is a man, therefore he is mortal." The assumed premise: "All men are mortal."

Thus, every utterance in the business of life is an objective social enthymeme. It is something like a "password" known only to those who belong to the same social purview. The distinguishing characteristic of behavioral utterances consists precisely in the fact that they make myriad connections with the extraverbal context of life and, once severed from that context, lose almost all their import—a person ignorant of the immediate pragmatic context will not understand these utterances.

This immediate context may be of varying scope. In our example, the context is extremely narrow: It is *circumscribed by the room and the moment of occurrence*, and the utterance makes an intelligible statement only for the two persons involved. However, the unified purview on which an utterance depends can expand in both space and time. *The "assumed" may be that of the family, clan, nation, class and may encompass days or years or whole epochs.* The wider the overall purview and its corresponding social group, the more *constant* the assumed factors in an utterance become.

When the assumed real purview of an utterance is narrow, when, as in our example, it coincides with the actual purview of two people sitting in the same room and seeing the same thing, then even the most momentary change within that purview can become the assumed. Where the purview is wider, the utterance can operate only on the basis of constant, stable factors in life and substantive, fundamental social evaluations.

Especially great importance, in this case, belongs to assumed evaluations. The fact is that all the basic social evaluations that stem directly from the distinctive characteristics of the given social group's economic being are usually not articulated. They have entered the flesh and blood of all representatives of the group; they organize behavior and actions; they have merged, as it were, with the objects and phenomena to which they correspond, and for that reason they are in no need of special verbal formulation. We seem to perceive the value of a thing together with its being as one of its qualities, we seem, for instance, to sense, along with its warmth and light, the sun's value for us, as well. All the phenomena that surround us are similarly merged with value judgments. If a value judgment is in actual fact conditioned by the being of a given community, it becomes a matter of dogmatic belief, something taken for granted and not subject to discussion. On the contrary, whenever some basic value judgment is verbalized and justified, we may be certain that if has already become dubious, has separated from its referent, has ceased to organize life, and, consequently, has lost its connection with the existential conditions of the given group.

A healthy social value judgment remains within life and from that position organizes the very form of an utterance and its intonation, but it does not at all aim to find suitable expression in the content side of discourse. Once a value judgment shifts from formal factors to content, we may be sure that a reevaluation is in the offing. Thus, a viable value judgment exists wholly without incorporation into the content of discourse and is not derivable therefrom; instead, it determines the *very selection of the verbal material and the form of the verbal whole*. It finds its purest expression in *intonation*. Intonation establishes a firm link between verbal discourse and the extraverbal context—genuine, living intonation moves verbal discourse beyond the border of the verbal, so to speak.

Let us stop to consider in somewhat greater detail the connection between intonation and the pragmatic context of life in the example utterance we have been using. This will allow us to make a number of important observations about the social nature of intonation.

IV

First of all, we must emphasize that the word *well*—a word virtually empty semantically—cannot to any extent predetermine intonation through its own content. Any intonation—joyful, sorrowful, contemptuous, and so on—can freely and easily operate in this word; it all depends on the context in which the word appears. In our example, the context determining the intonation used (indignant-reproachful but moderated by humor) is provided entirely by the extraverbal situation that we have already analyzed, since, in this instance, there is no immediate verbal context. We might say in advance that even were such an immediate verbal context present and even, moreover, if that context were entirely sufficient from all other points of view, the intonation would still take us beyond its confines. Intonation can be thoroughly understood only when one is in touch with the assumed value judgments of the given social group, whatever the scope of that group might be. *Intonation always lies on the border of the verbal and the nonverbal, the said and the unsaid*. In intonation, discourse comes directly into contact with life. And it is in intonation above all that the speaker comes into contact with the listener or listeners—intonation is social par excellence. It is especially sensitive to all the vibrations in the social atmosphere surrounding the speaker.

The intonation in our example stemmed from the interlocutors' shared yearning for spring and shared disgruntlement over the protracted winter. This commonness of evaluations assumed between them supplied the basis for the intonation, the basis for the distinctness and certitude of its major tonality. Given an atmosphere of sympathy, the intonation could freely undergo deployment and differentiation within the range of the major tone. But if there were no such firmly dependable "choral support," the intonation would have gone in a different direction and taken on different tones—perhaps those of provocation or annoyance with the listener, or perhaps the intonation would simply have contracted and been reduced to the minimum. When a person anticipates the disagreement of his interlocutor or, at any rate, is uncertain or doubtful of his agreement, he intones his words differently. We shall see later that not only intonation but the whole formal structure of speech depends to a significant degree on what the relation of the utterance is to the assumed community of values belonging to the social milieu wherein the discourse figures. A creatively productive, assured, and rich intonation is possible only on the basis of presupposed "choral support." Where such support is lacking, the voice falters and its intonational richness is reduced, as happens, for instance, when a person laughing suddenly realizes that he is laughing alone—his laughter either ceases or degenerates, becomes forced, loses its assurance and clarity and its ability to generate joking and amusing talk. *The commonness of assumed basic value judgments constitutes the canvas upon which living human speech embroiders the designs of intonation.*

Intonation's set toward possible sympathy, toward "choral support," does not exhaust its social nature. It is only one side of intonation—the side turned toward the listener. But intonation contains yet another extremely important factor for the sociology of discourse.

If we scrutinize the intonation of our example, we will notice that it has one "mysterious" feature requiring special explanation.

In point of fact, the intonation of the word *well* voiced not only passive dissatisfaction with an occurring event (the snowfall) but also active indignation and reproach. To whom is this reproach addressed? Clearly not to the listener but to somebody else. This tack of the intonational movement patently makes an opening in the situation for a *third participant*. Who is this third participant? Who is the recipient of the reproach? The snow? Nature? Fate, perhaps?

Of course, in our simplified example of a behavioral utterance the third participant—the "hero" of this verbal production—has not yet assumed full and definitive shape; the intonation has demarcated a definite place for the hero but his semantic equivalent has not been supplied and he remains nameless. Intonation has established an active attitude toward the referent, toward the object of the utterance, an attitude of a kind verging on *apostrophe* to that object as the incarnate, living culprit, while the listener—the second participant—is, as it were, called in *as witness and ally*.

Almost any example of live intonation in emotionally charged behavioral speech proceeds as if it addressed, behind inanimate objects and phenomena, animate participants and agents in life; in other words, it has an inherent *tendency toward personification*. If the intonation is not held in check, as in our example, by a certain amount of irony, then it becomes the source of the mythological image, the incantation, the prayer, as was the case in the earliest stages of culture. In our case, however, we have to do with an extremely important phenomenon of language creativity—*the intonational metaphor*. The intonation of the utterance "Well!" makes the word sound as if it were reproaching the living culprit of the late snowfall—winter. We have in our example an instance of *pure* intonational metaphor wholly confined within the intonation; but latent within it, in cradle, so to speak, there exists the possibility of the usual *semantic metaphor*. Were this possibility to be realized, the word *well* would expand into some such metaphorical expression as: "What a *stubborn winter! It just won't give up*, though goodness knows it's time!" But this possibility, inherent in the intonation, remained unrealized and the utterance made do with the almost semantically inert adverb *well*.

It should be noted that the intonation in behavioral speech, on the whole, is a great deal more metaphorical than the words used. The aboriginal myth-making spirit seems to have remained alive in it. Intonation makes it sound as if the world surrounding the speaker were still full of animate forces—it threatens and rails against or adores and cherishes inanimate objects and phenomena, whereas the usual metaphors of colloquial speech for the most part have been effaced and the words become semantically spare and prosaic.

Close kinship unites the intonational metaphor with the *gesticulatory metaphor* (indeed, words were themselves originally lingual gestures constituting one component of a complex, omnicorporeal gesture)—the term "gesture" being understood here in a broad sense, including miming as facial gesticulation. Gesture, just as intonation, requires the choral support of surrounding persons; only in an atmosphere of sympathy is free and assured gesture possible. Furthermore, and again just as intonation, gesture makes an opening in the situation and introduces a third participant—the hero. Gesture always has latent within itself the germ of attack or defence, of threat or caress, with the contemplator and listener relegated to the role of ally or witness. Often, the "hero" is merely some inanimate thing, some occurrence or circumstance in life. How often we shake our fist at "someone" in a fit of temper or simply scowl at empty space, and there is literally nothing we cannot smile at—the sun, trees, thoughts.

A point that must constantly be kept in mind (something that psychological aesthetics often forgets to do) is this: *Intonation and gesture are active and objective by tendency*. They not only express the passive mental state of the speaker but also always have embedded in them a living, forceful relation with the external world and with the social milieu—enemies, friends, allies. When a person intones and gesticulates, he assumes an active social position with respect to certain specific values, and this position is conditioned by the very bases of his social being. It is precisely this objective and sociological, and not subjective and psychological, aspect of intonation and gesture that should interest theorists of the various relevant arts, inasmuch as it is here that reside forces in the arts that are responsible for aesthetic creativity and that devise and organize artistic form.

As we see then, every instance of intonation is oriented *in two directions*: with respect to the listener as ally or witness and with respect to the object of the utterance as the third, living participant whom the intonation scolds or caresses, denigrates or magnifies. *This double social orientation is what determines all aspects of intonation and makes it intelligible.* And this very same thing is true for all the other factors of verbal utterances. They are all organized and in every way given shape in the same process of the speaker's *double orientation;* this social origin is only most easily detectable in intonation since it is the verbal factor of greatest sensitivity, elasticity, and freedom.

Thus, as we now have a right to claim, *any locution actually said aloud or written down for intelligible communication* (i.e., anything but words merely reposing in a dictionary) *is the expression and product of the social interaction of three participants: the speaker* (author), *the listener* (reader), and *the topic* (the who or what) *of speech* (the hero). Verbal discourse is a social event; it is not self-contained in the sense of some abstract linguistic quantity, nor can it be derived psychologically from the speaker's subjective consciousness taken in isolation. Therefore, both the formal linguistic approach and the psychological approach equally miss the mark. The concrete, sociological essence of verbal discourse, that which alone can make it true or false, banal or distinguished, necessary or unnecessary, remains beyond the ken and reach of both these points of view. Needless to say, it is also this very same "social soul" of verbal discourse that makes it beautiful or ugly, that is, that makes it artistically meaningful, as well. To be sure, once subordinated to the basic and more concrete sociological approach, both abstract points of view—the formal linguistic and the psychological—retain their value. Their collaboration is even absolutely indispensable; but separately, each by itself in isolation, they are inert.

The concrete utterance (and not the linguistic abstraction) is born, lives, and dies in the process of social interaction between the participants of the utterance. Its form and meaning are determined basically by the form and character of this interaction. When we cut the utterance off from the real grounds that nurture it, we lose the key to its form as well as to its import—all we have left is an abstract linguistic shell or an equally abstract semantic scheme (the banal "idea of the work" with which earlier theorists and historians of literature dealt)—two abstractions that are not mutually joinable because there are no concrete grounds for their organic synthesis.

It remains for us now only to sum up our short analysis of utterance in life and of those *artistic potentials, those rudiments of future form and content*, that we have detected in it.

The meaning and import of an utterance in life (of whatever particular kind that utterance may be) do not coincide with the purely verbal composition of the utterance. Articulated words are impregnated with assumed and unarticulated qualities. What are called the "understanding" and "evaluation" of an utterance (agreement or disagreement) always encompass the extraverbal pragmatic situation together with the verbal discourse proper. Life, therefore, does not affect an utterance from without; it penetrates and exerts an influence on an utterance from within, as that unity and commonness of being surrounding the speakers and that unity and commonness of essential social value judgments issuing from that being without all of which no intelligible utterance is possible. Intonation lies on the border between life and the verbal aspect of the utterance; it, as it were, pumps energy from a life situation into tne verbal discourse, it endows everything linguistically stable with living historical momentum and uniqueness. Finally, the utterance reflects the social interaction of the speaker, listener, and hero as the product and fixation in verbal material of the act of living communication among them.

Verbal discourse is like a *"scenario"* of a certain event. A viable understanding of the whole import of discourse must *reproduce* this event of the mutual relationship between speakers, must, as it were, "reenact" it, with the person wishing to understand taking upon himself the role of the listener. But in order to carry out that role, he must distinctly understand the positions of the other two participants, as well.

For the linguistic point of view, neither this event nor its living participants exist, of course; the linguistic point of view deals with abstract, bare words and their equally abstract components (phonetic, morphological, and so on). Therefore, the *total import of discourse* and *its ideological value*—the cognitive, political, aesthetic, or other—are inaccessible to it. Just as there cannot be a linguistic logic or a linguistic politics, so there cannot be a linguistic poetics.

V

In what way does an artistic verbal utterance—a complete work of poetic art—differ from an utterance in the business of life?

It is immediately obvious that discourse in art neither is nor can be so closely dependent on all the factors of the extraverbal context, on all that is seen and known, as in life. A poetic work cannot rely on objects and events in the immediate milieu as things "understood" without making even the slightest allusion to them in the verbal part of the utterance. In this regard, a great deal more is demanded of discourse in literature: Much that could remain outside the utterance in life must find verbal representation. Nothing must be left unsaid in a poetic work from the pragmatic-referential point of view.

Does it follow from this that in literature the speaker, listener, and hero come in contact for the first time, knowing nothing about one another, having no purview in common, and are, therefore, bereft of anything on which they can jointly rely or hold assumptions about? Certain writers on these topics are inclined to think so.

But in actuality a poetic work, too, is closely enmeshed in the unarticulated context of life. If it were true that author, listener, and hero, as abstract persons, come into contact for the first time devoid of any unifying purview and that the words used are taken as from a dictionary, then it is hardly likely that even a nonpoetic work would result, and certainly not a poetic one. Science does to some degree approach this extreme—a scientific definition has a minimum of the "assumed"; but it would be possible to prove that even science cannot do entirely without the assumed.

In literature, assumed value judgments play a role of particular importance. We might say that *a poetic work is a powerful condenser of unarticulated social evaluations*—each word is saturated with them. *It is these social evaluations that organize form as their direct expression.*

Value judgments, first of all, determine the author's *selection of words* and the reception of that selection (the coselection) by the listener. The poet, after all, selects words not from the dictionary but from the context of life where words have been steeped in and become permeated with value judgments. Thus, he selects the value judgments associated with the words and does so, moreover, from the standpoint of the incarnated bearers of those value judgments. It can be said that the poet constantly works in conjunction with his listener's sympathy or antipathy, agreement or disagreement. Furthermore, evaluation is operative also with regard to the object of the utterance—the hero. The simple selection of an epithet or a metaphor is already an active evaluative act with orientation in both directions—toward the listener and toward the hero. *Listener and hero are constant participants in the creative event*, which does not for a single instant cease to be an event of living communication involving all three.

The problem of sociological poetics would be resolved if each factor of form could be explained as the active expression of evaluation in these two directions—toward the listener and toward the object of utterance, the hero.[6] But at the present time the data are too insufficient for such a task to be carried out. All that can be done is to map out at least the preliminary steps leading toward that goal.

The formalistic aesthetics of the present day defines artistic forms as *the form of the material.* If this point of view be carried out consistently, content must necessarily be ignored, since no room is left for it in the poetic work; at best, it may be regarded as a factor of the material and in that way, indirectly, be organized by artistic form in its direct bearing on the material.[7]

So understood, form loses its active evaluative character and becomes merely a stimulus of passive feelings of pleasure in the perceiver.

It goes without saying that form is realized with the help of the material—it is fixed in material; but by virtue of *its significance* it exceeds the material. *The*

---

[6] We ignore technical questions of form here but will have something to say on this topic later.

[7] The point of view of V. M. Žirmunskij.

meaning, the import of form has to do not with the material but with the content. So, for instance, the form of a statue may be said to be not the form of the marble but the form of the human body, with the added qualification that the form "heroicizes" the human depicted or "dotes upon" him or, perhaps, denigrates him (the caricature style in the plastic arts); that is, the form expresses some specific evaluation of the object depicted.

The evaluative significance of form is especially obvious in verse. Rhythm and other formal elements of verse overtly express a certain active attitude toward the object depicted: The form celebrates or laments or ridicules that object.

Psychological aesthetics calls this the "emotional factor" of form. But it is not the psychological side of the matter that is important for us, not the identity of the psychical forces that take part in the creation of form and the cocreative perception of form. What is important is the significance of these experiences, their active role, their bearing on content. Through the agency of artistic form the creator takes up *an active position with respect to content.* The form in and of itself need not necessarily be pleasurable (the hedonistic explanation of form is absurd); what it must be is a *convincing evaluation* of the content. So, for instance, while the form of "the enemy" might even be repulsive, the positive state, the pleasure that the contemplator derives in the end, is a consequence of the fact that the form is *appropriate to the enemy* and that it is *technically perfect* in its realization through the agency of the material. It is in these two aspects that form should be studied: with respect to content, as its ideological evaluation, and with respect to the material, as the technical realization of that evaluation.

The ideological evaluation expressed through form is not at all supposed to transpose into content as a maxim or a proposition of a moral, political, or other kind. The evaluation should remain in the rhythm, *in the very evaluative impetus* of the epithet or metaphor, *in the manner of the unfolding* of the depicted event; it is supposed to be realized by the formal means of the material only. But, at the same time, while not transposing into content, the form must not lose its connection with content, its correlation with it, otherwise it becomes a technical experiment devoid of any real artistic import.

The general definition of style that classical and neoclassical poetics had advanced, together with the basic division of style into "high" and "low," aptly brings out precisely this active evaluative nature of artistic form. The structure of form is indeed *hierarchical,* and in this respect it comes close to political and juridical gradations. Form similarly creates, in an artistically configured content, a complex system of hierarchical interrelations. Each of its elements—an epithet or a metaphor, for instance—either raises the designatum to a higher degree or lowers it or equalizes it. The selection of a hero or an event determines from the very outset the general level of the form and the admissibility of this or that particular set of configurating devices. And this basic requirement of *stylistic suitability* has in view *the evaluative-hierarchical suitability of form and content*: They must be *equally adequate* for one another. The selection of content and the selection of form constitute one and the same act establishing the creator's basic position; and in that act one and the same social evaluation finds expression.

VI

Sociological analysis can take its starting point only, of course, from the purely verbal, linguistic makeup of a work, but it must not and cannot confine itself within those limits, as linguistic poetics does. Artistic contemplation via the reading of a poetic work does, to be sure, start from the grapheme (the visual image of written or printed words), but at the very instant of perception this visual image gives way to and is very nearly obliterated by other verbal factors—articulation, sound image, intonation, meaning—and these factors eventually take us beyond the border of the verbal altogether. And so it can be said that *the purely linguistic factor of a work is to the artistic whole as the grapheme is to the verbal whole*. In poetry, as in life, verbal discourse is a *"scenario" of an event*. Competent artistic perception reenacts it, sensitively surmising from the words and the forms of their organization the specific, living interrelations of the author with the world he depicts and entering into those interrelations as a third participant (the listener's role). Where linguistic analysis sees only words and the interrelations of their abstract factors (phonetic, morphological, syntactic, and so on), there, for living artistic perception and for concrete sociological analysis, relations among *people* stand revealed, relations merely reflected and fixed in verbal material. Verbal discourse is the skeleton that takes on living flesh only in the process of creative perception—consequently, only in the process of living social communication.

In what follows here we shall attempt to provide a brief and preliminary sketch of the essential factors in the interrelationships of the participants in an artistic event—those factors that determine the broad and basic lines of poetic style as a social phenomenon. Any further detailing of these factors would, of course, go beyond the scope of the present essay.

The author, hero, and listener that we have been talking about all this time are to be understood not as entities outside the artistic event but only as entities of the very perception of an artistic work, entities that are essential constitutive factors of the work. They are the living forces that determine form and style and are distinctly detectable by any competent contemplator. This means that all those definitions that a historian of literature and society mighty apply to the author and his heroes—the author's biography, the precise qualifications of heroes in chronological and sociological terms and so on—are excluded here: They do not enter directly into the structure of the work but remain outside it. The listener, too, is taken here as the listener whom the author himself takes into account, the one toward whom the work is oriented and who, consequently, intrinsically determines the work's structure. Therefore, we do not at all mean the actual people who in fact made up the reading public of the author in question.

The first form-determining factor of content is the *evaluative rank* of the depicted event and its agent—the hero (whether named or not), taken in strict correlation with the rank of the creator and contemplator. Here we have to do, just as in legal or political life, with a *two-sided relationship*: master-slave, ruler-subject, comrade-comrade, and the like.

The basic stylistic tone of an utterance is therefore determined above all by who is talked about and what his relation is to the speaker—whether he is higher or lower than or equal to him on the scale of the social hierarchy. King, father, brother, slave, comrade, and so on, as heroes of an utterance, also determine its formal structure. And this *specific hierarchical weight* of the hero is determined, in its turn, by that unarticulated context of basic evaluations in which a poetic work, too, participates. Just as the "intonational metaphor" in our example utterance from life established an organic relationship with the object of the utterance, so also all elements of the style of a poetic work are permeated with the author's evaluative attitude toward content and express his basic social position. Let us stress once again that we have in mind here not those ideological evaluations that are incorporated into the content of a work in the form of judgments or conclusions but that deeper, more ingrained kind of *evaluation via form* that finds expression in the very manner in which the artistic material is viewed and deployed.

Certain languages, Japanese in particular, possess a rich and varied store of special lexical and grammatical forms to be used in strict accordance with the rank of the hero of the utterance (language etiquette).[8]

We might say that what is still a *matter of grammar* for the Japanese has already become for us a *matter of style*. The most important stylistic components of the heroic epic, the tragedy, the ode, and so forth are determined precisely by the hierarchical status of the object of the utterance with respect to the speaker.

It should not be supposed that this hierarchical interdefinition of creator and hero has been eliminated from modern literature. It has been made more complex and does not reflect the contemporary sociopolitical hierarchy with the same degree of distinctness as, say, classicism did in its time—but *the very principle of change of style in accordance with change in the social value of the hero of the utterance* certainly remains in force as before. After all, it is not his personal enemy that the poet hates, not his personal friend that his form treats

[8] See W. Humboldt, *Kawi-Werk* No. 2:335, and Hoffman, *Japan. Sprachlehre*, p. 75.

with love and tenderness, not the events from his private life that he rejoices or sorrows over. Even if a poet has in fact borrowed his passion in good measure from the circumstances of his own private life, still, he must *socialize* that passion and, consequently, elaborate the event with which it corresponds to the level of *social significance*.

The second style-determining factor in the interrelationship between hero and creator is *the degree of their proximity to one another*. All languages possess direct grammatical means of expression for this aspect: first, second, and third persons and variable sentence structure in accordance with the person of the subject ("I" or "you" or "he"). The form of a proposition about a third person, the form of an address to a second person, the form of an utterance about oneself (and their modifications) are already different in terms of grammar. Thus, here *the very structure of the language reflects the event of the speakers' interrelationship*.

Certain languages have purely grammatical forms capable of conveying with even greater flexibility the nuances of the speakers' social interrelationship and the various degrees of their proximity. From this angle, the so-called "inclusive" and "exclusive" forms of the plural in certain languages present a case of special interest. For example, if a speaker using the form *we* has the listener in mind and includes him in the subject of the proposition, then he uses one form, whereas if he means himself and some other person (*we* in the sense of *I* and *he*), he uses a different form. Such is the use of the dual in certain Australian languages, for instances. There, too, are found two special forms of the triad: one meaning *I and you and he*; the other, *I and he and he* (with *you*—the listener—excluded).

In European languages these and similar interrelationships between speakers have no special grammatical expression. The character of these languages is more abstract and not so capable of reflecting the situation of utterance via grammatical structure. However, interrelationships between speakers do find expression in these languages—and expression of far greater subtlety and diversity—*in the style and intonation of utterances*. Here the social situation of creativity finds thoroughgoing reflection in a work by means of purely artistic devices.

The form of a poetic work is determined, therefore, in many of its factors by *how the author perceives his hero*—the hero who serves as the organizing center of the utterance. The form of *objective narration*, the form of *address or apostrophe* (prayer, hymn, certain lyric forms), the form of *self-expression* (confession, autobiography, lyric avowal—an important form of the love lyric) are determined precisely by the *degree of proximity between author and hero*.

Both the factors we have indicated—the hierarchical value of the hero and the degree of his proximity to the author—are as yet insufficient, taken indepen-

[9] See Matthews, *Aboriginal Languages of Victoria*. Also, Humboldt, *Kawi-Werk*.

dently and in isolation, for the determination of artistic form. The fact is that a third participant is constantly in play as well—the listener, whose presence affects the interrelationship of the other two (creator and hero).

The interrelationship of author and hero never, after all, actually is an intimate relationship of two; all the while form makes provision for the third participant—the listener—who exerts crucial influence on all the other factors of the work.

In what way can the listener determine the style of a poetic utterance? Here, too, we must distinguish two basic factors: first, the listener's proximity to the author and, second, his relation to the hero. Nothing is more perilous for aesthetics than to ignore the autonomous role of the listener. A very commonly held opinion has it that the listener is to be regarded as equal to the author, excepting the latter's technical performance, and that the position of a competent listener is supposed to be a simple reproduction of the author's position. In actual fact this is not so. Indeed, the opposite may sooner be said to be true: The listener never equals the author. The listener has *his own independent place* in the event of artistic creation; he must occupy a special, and, what is more, a *two-sided* position in it—with respect to the author and with respect to the hero—and it is this position that has determinative effect on the style of an utterance.

How does the author sense his listener? In our example of an utterance in the business of life, we have seen to what degree the presumed agreement or disagreement of the listener shaped an utterance. Exactly the same is true regarding all factors of form. To put it figuratively, the listener normally stands *side by side* with the author as his ally, but this classical positioning of the listener is by no means always the case.

Sometimes the listener begins to lean toward the hero of the utterance. The most unmistakable and typical expression of this is the polemical style that aligns the hero and the listener together. Satire, too, can involve the listener as someone calculated to be close to the hero ridiculed and not to the ridiculing author. This constitutes a sort of *inclusive form of ridicule* distinctly different from the exclusive form where the listener is in solidarity with the jeering author. In romanticism, an interesting phenomenon can be observed where the author *concludes an alliance*, as it were, *with his hero against the listener* (Friedrich Schlegel's *Lucinda* and, in Russian literature, *Hero of Our Time* to some extent).

Of very special character and interest for analysis is the author's sense of his listener in the forms of the confession and the autobiography. All shades of feeling from humble reverence before the listener, as before a veritable judge, to contemptuous distrust and hostility can have determinative effect on the style of a confession or an autobiography. Extremely interesting material for the illustration of this contention can be found in the works of Dostoevskij. The confessional style of

Ippolit's "article" (*The Idiot*) is determined by an almost extreme degree of contemptuous distrust and hostility directed toward all who are to hear this dying confession. Similar tones, but somewhat softened, determine the style of *Notes from Underground*. The style of "Stavrogin's Confession" (*The Possessed*) displays far greater trust in the listener and acknowledgments of his rights, although here too, from time to time, a feeling almost of hatred for the listener erupts, which is what is responsible for the jaggedness of its style. Playing the fool, as a special form of utterance, one, to be sure, lying on the periphery of the artistic, is determined above all by an extremely complex and tangled conflict of the speaker with the listener.

A form especially sensitive to the position of the listener is the lyric. The underlying condition for lyric intonation is *the absolute certainty of the listener's sympathy*. Should any doubt on this score creep into the lyric situation, the style of the lyric changes drastically. This conflict with the listener finds its most egregious expression in so-called lyric irony (Heine, and in modern poetry, Laforgue, Annenskij, and others). The form of irony in general is conditioned by a social conflict: It is the encounter in one voice of two incarnate value judgments and their interference with one another.

In modern aesthetics a special, so-called juridical theory of tragedy was proposed, a theory amounting essentially to the attempt to conceive of *the structure of a tragedy as the structure of a trial in court*.[10]

The interrelationship of hero and chorus, on the one side, and the overall position of the listener, on the other, do indeed, to a degree, lend themselves to juridical interpretation. But of course this can only be meant as *an analogy*. The important common feature of tragedy—indeed of any work of art—and judicial process comes down merely to the existence of "sides," that is, the occupying by the several participants of *different positions*. The terms, so widespread in literary terminology, that define the poet as "judge," "exposer," "witness," "defender," and even "executioner" (the phraseology for "scourging satire"—Juvenal, Barbier, Nekrasov, and others), and associated definitions for heroes and listeners, reveal by way of analogy, the same social base of poetry. At all events, author, hero, and listener nowhere merge together into one indifferent mass—they occupy *autonomous positions*, they are indeed "sides," the sides not of a judicial process but of an artistic event with specific social structure the "protocol" of which is the work of art.

It would not be amiss at this point to stress once again that we have in mind, and have had in mind all this time, the listener as an immanent participant in the artistic event who has determinative effect on the form of the work from within. This listener, on a par with the author and the hero, is an essential, intrinsic

---

[10] For the most interesting development of this point of view, see Hermann Cohen, *Ästhetik des reinen Gefühls*, vol. 2.

factor of the work and does not at all coincide with the so-called reading public, located outside the work, whose artistic tastes and demands can be consciously taken into account. Such a conscious account is incapable of direct and pro- found effect on artistic form in the process of its living creation. What is more, if this conscious account of the reading public does come to occupy a position of any importance in a poet's creativity, that creativity inevitably loses its artistic purity and degrades to a lower social level.

This external account bespeaks the poet's loss of *his immanent listener*, his divorce from the *social whole* that *intrinsically*, aside from all abstract considera- tions, has the capability of determining *his value judgments* and the artistic form of his poetic utterances, which form is the expression of those crucial social value judgments. The more a poet is cut off from the social unity of his group, the more likely he is to take into account the *external* demands of a *particular reading public*. Only a social group alien to the poet can determine his creative work from outside. One's *own* group needs no such external definition. It exists in the poet's voice, in the basic tone and intonations of that voice—whether the poet himself intends this or not.

The poet acquires his words and learns to intone them *over the course of his entire life* in the process of his every-sided contact with his environment. The poet begins to use those words and intonations already in the *inner speech* with the help of which he thinks and becomes conscious of himself, even when he does not produce utterances. It is naive to suppose that one can assimilate as one's own *an external speech that runs counter to one's inner speech*, that is, runs counter to one's whole inner verbal manner of being aware of oneself and the world. Even if it is possible to create such a thing for some pragmatic occasion, still, as something cut off from all sources of sustenance, it will be devoid of any artistic productiveness. A poet's style is engendered from *the style of his inner speech*, which does not lend itself to control, and his inner speech is itself the product of his entire social life. "Style is the man," they say; but we might say: Style is at least two persons or, more accurately, one person plus his social group in the form of its authoritative representative, the listener—the constant participant in a person's inner and outward speech.

The fact of the matter is that no conscious act of any degree of distinctness can do without inner speech, without words and intonations—without evalua- tions, and, consequently, every conscious act is already a social act, an act of communication. Even the most intimate self-awareness is an attempt to translate oneself into the common code, to take stock of another's point of view, and, consequently, entails orientation toward a possible listener. This listener may be only the bearer of the value judgments of the social group to which the "conscious" person belongs. In this regard, consciousness, provided that we do not lose sight of its content, is *not just a psychological phenomenon* but also, and above all, an *ideological phenomenon, a product of social intercourse.* This constant *coparticipant* in all our conscious acts determines not only the content of consciousness but also—and this is the main point for us—the very *selection* of the content, the selection of what precisely we become conscious of, and thus determines also those *evaluations* which permeate consciousness and which psychology usually calls the "emotional tone" of consciousness. It is precisely from this constant participant in all our conscious acts that the listener who determines artistic form is engendered.

There is nothing more perilous than to conceive of this subtle social structure of verbal creativity as analogous with the conscious and cynical speculations of the bourgeois publisher who "calculates the prospects of the book market," and to apply to the characterization of the immanent structure of a work categories of the "supply-demand" type. Alas, all too many "sociologists" are likely to identify the creative writer's service to society with the vocation of the enterprising publisher.

Under the conditions of the bourgeois economy, the book market does, of course, "regulate" writers, but this is not in any way to be identified with the regulative role of the listener as a constant structural element in artistic creativity. For a historian of the literature of the capitalist era, the market is a very important factor, but for theoretical poetics, which studies the basic ideological structure of art, that external factor is irrelevant. However, even in the historical study of literature the history of the book market must not be confused with the history of literature.

VII

All the form-determining factors of an artistic utterance that we have analyzed—(1) the hierarchical value of the hero or event serving as the content of the utterance, (2) the degree of the latter's proximity to the author, and (3) the listener and his interrelationship with the author, on the one side, and the hero, on the other—all those factors are *the contact points between the social forces of extraartistic reality and verbal art*. Thanks precisely to that kind of *intrinsically social structure* which artistic creation possesses, it is *open on all sides to the influence of other domains of life*. Other ideological spheres, prominently including the sociopolitical order and the economy, have determinative effect on verbal art not merely from outside but with direct bearing upon its intrinsic structural elements. And, conversely, the artistic interaction of author, listener, and hero may exert its influence on other domains of social intercourse.

Full and thoroughgoing elucidation of questions as to who the typical heroes of literature at some particular period are, what the typical formal orientation of the author toward them is, what the interrelationships of the author and hero with the listener are in the whole of an artistic creation—elucidation of such questions presupposes thoroughgoing analysis of the economic and ideological conditions of the time.

But these concrete historical issues exceed the scope of theoretical poetics which, however, still does include one other important task. Up to now we have been concerned only with those factors which determine form in its relation to content, that is, form as the embodied social evaluation of precisely that content, and we have ascertained that every factor of form is a product of social interaction. But we also pointed out that form must be understood from another angle, as well—as form realized with the help of *specific material.* This opens up a whole long series of questions connected with *the technical aspect of form.*

Of course, *these technical questions can be separated out from questions of the sociology of form only in abstract terms; in actuality* it is impossible to divorce the *artistic import* of some device, say, a metaphor that relates to content and expresses the formal evaluation of it (i.e., the metaphor degrades the object or raises it to a higher rank), from *the purely linguistic* specification of that device.

The extraverbal import of a metaphor—a regrouping of values—and *its linguistic covering*—a semantic shift—are merely different points of view on one and the same real phenomenon. But the second point of view is subordinate to the first. A poet uses a metaphor in order to regroup values and not for the sake of a linguistic exercise.

All questions of form can be taken in relation with material—in the given case, in relation with language in its linguistic conception. Technical analysis will then amount to the question as to *which linguistic means are used for the realization of the socioartistic purpose of the form.* But if that purpose is not known, if its import is not elucidated in advance, technical analysis will be absurd.

Technical questions of form, of course, go beyond the scope of the task we have set ourself here. Moreover, their treatment would require an incomparably more diversified and elaborated analysis of the socioartistic aspect of verbal art. Here we have been able to provide only a brief sketch of the basic directions such an analysis must take.

If we have succeeded in demonstrating even the mere possibility of a sociological approach to the immanent structure of poetic form, we may consider our task to have been fulfilled.

A Critique of Marxist Apologias of Freudianism

V. N. Vološinov

1. Marxism and Freudianism. 2. Bykhovskii's viewpoint. 3. Luria's viewpoint. 4. Fridman's viewpoint. 5. Zalkind's reflexologized Freudianism. 6. Summation.

I

The reader who has been closely following this discussion of Freudianism will no doubt have already developed the feeling, all critical analysis aside, that this doctrine is profoundly, structurally foreign to Marxism. It is difficult not to sense the completely different atmosphere, the different perspective, of the Freudian world view. There are, nevertheless, some ardent Marxist apologists of Freudianism. I have had cause to mention them previously, in the early, introductory chapters of this work. Here, at the conclusion of the critical portion of this book, I cannot shirk the rather thankless task of subjecting these Marxist apologias of Freudianism to an analytical critique.

I cannot, of course, dwell upon all the "receptive" and "well-disposed" statements and comments that Marxists have made about Freudianism. Frequently, statements such as these are haphazard, are not thoroughly developed or substantiated. This category includes Comrade Trotsky's famous dictum (in his book *Literature and revolution* [Literatura i revoliutsiia]) on Marxism's ability to accommodate psychoanalysis. Such statements will not detain us here. I shall limit myself to an examination of the works of four writers:

V. N. Voloshinov, *Freidizm: kriticheskii ocherk* (Moscow-Leningrad, 1927), chapter 10. The translation is by Liv Tudge. Reprinted from *Soviet Psychology*, Vol. XXIII, No. 3, Spring 1985, by permission of M. E. Sharpe, Inc., Armonk, NY 10504. The terminology and transliteration of the original publication have been retained.

(1) an article by B. Bykhovskii, in a 1923 issue of *Pod znamenem marksizma*, entitled "Concerning the methodological underpinnings of Freud's psychoanalytical doctrine";

(2) A. R. Luria's article "Psychoanalysis as a system of monistic psychology," in the anthology *Psychology and Marxism* [Psikhologiya i Marksizm] [edited by K. P. Kornilov] (Moscow Institute of Experimental Psychology, 1925);

(3) B. D. Fridman's "Freud's fundamental psychological views and the theory of historical materialism," published in the above-mentioned volume;

(4) A. B. Zalkind's article "Freudianism and Marxism," in the journal *Krasnaia Nov'*, 1924, No. 4, and the relevant chapters of his most recent book *Suggestion and the life of the organism*, [Zhizn' organizma i vnushenie] (1927).

These works are the most fully developed and considered attempts to justify Freudianism from a Marxist point of view. By inquiring into these writers' apologetics we largely exhaust all the arguments of any note that Marxists have advanced in defense of Freudianism.

II

We shall work in chronological order, beginning with a critique of Bykhovskii's piece.

> The psychoanalytical doctrine is enveloped in a dense integument of subjectivism; and phenomena, as discussed by psychoanalysts, frequently appear to have been turned "subjective-side out." But I have endeavored to bare the sound kernel of psychoanalysis, and believe it to be of tolerable value and significance. I have endeavored to prove that, in methodological premises and basic, fundamental conclusions, psychoanalysis reiterates (unconsciously) in its research the tenets propounded by dialectical materialism. A grasp of this fact on the part of psychoanalysts will place their doctrine upon a broad and firm foundation. Dialectical materialism can then record another victory to its credit. (Pp. 176–77)

Thus does Bykhovskii sum up his analysis of Freudianism.

In what, though, does he descry the "sound kernel" of psychoanalysis, which "reiterates unconsciously" the tenets of dialectical materialism?

Bykhovskii sets out to prove that the characteristic elements of the psychoanalytical method are: objectivism, materialist monism, energeticism, and, finally, the dialectic.

I shall analyze these attributes of Freudian methodology as elucidated by Bykhovskii point by point.

Bykhovskii has an exceedingly odd way of substantiating the objectivism of the Freudian method. Let us cite his own words:

> Upon closer familiarity with psychoanalysis, one not only becomes convinced of the extent of its compatibility with reactology but one also begins to harbor doubts concerning its subjectivism. Subjectivism is the integument that obscures the main point. In actual fact, psychoanalysis is the doctrine of the unconscious, of something that occurs

beyond the bounds of the subjective ego. The unconscious has a real effect upon the organism's reactions, and sometimes guides them. *The unconscious cannot be studied subjectively, through consciousness.* This explains why Freud studies the *objective manifestations* of the unconscious (a symptom, a slip and so on), seeks out states in which the participation of consciousness is minimal (sleep, childhood). All this is assuredly acceptable to reactology. (P. 166)

Bykhovskii's assertions run counter to the very bases of Freudian methodology. Freud himself stated, "We can learn of the unconscious only through consciousness." The entire methodology of "free association" has a single aim: to draw the unconscious into the patient's consciousness. And psychoanalytic theory will be successful, according to Freud, if—and only if—the patient *himself*, through his own *internal experience*, recognizes and acknowledges his displaced complexes.[1] If the patient were to continue to regard them as merely external, objective facts, bereft for him of the *subjective authenticity* that attaches to the internally experienced, they would have no therapeutic import whatever. We apprehend, for instance, the image of a diseased lung on an X-ray plate, or learn about the physiological mechanism of coughing as an objective fact (residing outside the subjective psyche). But one will encounter the "unconscious" only along the subjective routes of internal experience. One must come upon it through one's internal experience, in the depths of one's mind. And the whole of psychoanalysis is nothing more than becoming *internally* aware of the unconscious. One fails to comprehend what grounds Bykhovskii has for asserting that "the unconscious cannot be studied subjectively, through consciousness"! There is not, nor could there be, any other way to study it; and Freud himself never so much as entertained any other possibility.

Furthermore, Bykhovskii's assertion that Freudianism studies the objective manifestations of the unconscious in a symptom or in a slip or the like is an outright falsehood. Of course, the Freudian analyst proceeds from the external, objective *donnée*—the somatic symptom, and so on—but he does not actually study that objective, material *donnée*. He is completely uninterested in the physiological mechanism of the somatic symptom (the hysterical cough, for instance); he is interested only in its internal, subjective-psychical obverse. The psychoanalytical method strips the symptom, the slip, the dream, and all other such facts from which it proceeds of their objective materiality, as it were. Psychoanalysis deals with them only as substitute formations, as a compromise position between consciousness and the unconscious—and, consequently, only as a particular combination of mental forces. *The symptom, in the psychoanalytic formulation, consists exclusively of purely subjective-mental quantities.*

How the psychoanalytic method—which seeks always and everywhere for the one precious gem, the displaced desire—can be an objective method acceptable to reactology remains quite beyond comprehension. Bykhovskii's "arguments" are simply an unsubstantiated assertion. And he adduces no others.

Substantiation of the second feature of psychoanalysis—its materialist monism—fares no better. Bykhovskii's basic argument here amounts to averring that the Freudian method creates an uninterrupted passage from the psyche to the soma by way of the unconscious (which results in a "consciousness-preconscious-unconscious-soma" nexus). He quotes Freud's famous assertion: "The sexual function is no more purely mental than it is merely somatic. It exerts an influence upon both corporeal and mental life" (p. 164). One could extract many analogous quotations from Freud, but it is possible to find even more assertions that run directly counter to this. Bykhovskii himself quotes one of these a little farther on, as follows:

> It is important to ascertain whether individual mental manifestations derive directly from physical, organic, material influences—in which case psychology has no business studying them—or whether the phenomena derive from and are connected with other mental processes, behind which, at some later point, a nexus of organic causes lies concealed. It is only processes of the "second order" that we habitually term mental processes. (P. 165)

Here, in this assertion, Freud jettisons everything organic from psychology. The psychoanalyst studies only the purely mental nexus; the rest does not concern him. But since "at some later point" the nexus of organic causes—which is nevertheless of interest to the psychologist—is admitted, what we have here is a typical expression of psychophysical parallelism. The position Freud himself adopts concerning the theoretical solution to the problem of the psychosomatic interrelationship is, in general, evasive and deliberately vague. All his statements, with any bearing on this are contradictory and indeterminate. More often than not, he avoids the question entirely. But there is no need to assemble these statements: the method speaks for itself—in practice, in the way it works. At no time and nowhere does psychoanalysis show us the impact of the soma on the psyche, as Bykhovskii would have it do. Psychoanalysis recognizes only the purely mental nexus; it recognizes the somatic only as a subordinate element of that mental nexus. Consistent psychoanalysts such as Rank and Groddeck have formulated a clear and unequivocal theoretical expression for this feature of their method: they are convinced that *everything organic* is *secondary in nature*; the mental alone predominates. This is unadulterated monism—but it is *spiritualistic monism*.

Psychoanalysis is, indeed, fundamentally monistic. It is a unique, modern variant of spiritualistic monism. Let the circumspect Freud maintain an ambiguous balance between psychophysical causality and psychophysical parallelism—the method itself knows no such ambiguity. In it there are no insuperable and impenetrable material quantities; in it everything dissolves into an infinite and unstable subjective-mental medium.

We proceed now to energetics, with a quotation from Bykhovskii himself:

> The compatibility of psychoanalysis and reactology goes beyond our previous discussion. It is considerably more profound, extending to the fundamental foundations of the theory—to the energeticism of mental processes. The energetic conception of mental processes permeates Freud's psychoanalytical doctrine from beginning to end. In

Freud, energetics is dubbed "the economic viewpoint." The one thing that may be confidently asserted is that pleasure is connected in some way with the diminution, reduction, or extinction of the total number of stimuli resident in the mental apparatus, and pain, with a rise in that number. Research into the most intense pleasure available to man—pleasure gained from completion of the sex act—leaves no room for doubt on this point. Since in such pleasure processes we are dealing with a reckoning of the quantity of mental stimuli or energy, we term reasoning of this kind "economic." . . . It can be said that the mental apparatus aims to conquer and to free itself from stimuli and excitations, apprehended both from within and from without. (Pp. 166–67)

Thus, with a quotation from Freud, Bykhovskii seeks to prove the psychoanalytic theory of the source of mental energy. The quotation is indeed typical, but it does not prove what Bykhovskii would have it prove.

What is this "economic viewpoint" in Freud? Simply a groundless transposition to the mind of a principle of "minimum expenditure of energy" that is as old as the hills. But when applied to subjectively mental material, that principle—which is in itself vacuous, and platitudinous to boot—becomes a mere metaphor, a poetic turn of phrase, and nothing more. That principle could serve as a productive working hypothesis only *for material that lends itself to precise objective measurement.* The subjective-mental, which is detached from everything material, does not, of course, lend itself to measurement of any kind, only to arbitrary Ideological assessments. One such dubious (to say the least) assessment is Freud's cynical declaration that the most intense pleasure available to man is the pleasure gained through completion of the sex act.

There can be no talk of energetics where there is no basis for precise measurement. The special attribute of Freud's theory is that it recognizes no objective *material stimulus*; it knows only internal—mental—stimuli. (Freud, it is true, speaks of the somatic wellsprings of instincts, but he does not study them.) The entire Freudian theory of the libido operates solely upon such internal stimuli. Freudianism's interest in the stimulus actually begins only at the point when that stimulus makes its appearance on the internal, mental stage and clashes with forces that are already in place there. How the stimulus got there is of no interest at all. Freud defines instincts (*die Triebe*)—the fundamental concept of all psychoanalysis—as the mental repercussions of somatic stimuli. And he is consistent in dealing only with those repercussions and the conflict between them: the mother instinct clashes with fear and shame, and is displaced into the unconsciousness; the ego instinct clashes with the sex instinct; the death instinct, with eros; and so forth. Psychoanalysis thus *remains within the ambit of intrapsychic stimuli and reactions*: experience reacts to experience, feeling to desire, desire to feeling. The mind reacts to incestuous love with fear, to the homosexual instinct with persecution mania, and so forth. The material stimulus in the outside world and the stimulus expressed materially in the organism remain beyond the bounds of this theory. Nevertheless, these *measurable* features provide a basis for psychology's objective methods.

The same, it must be said, applies to the conversion of mental energy: the transition of love to hate, the transference of an instinct from one object to another, and so on. How can this energy, being so inconstant in form, be quantified? Yet only in such a case would we be able to use the term *energetics* literally. But for that it is necessary to pass beyond the bounds of the subjectively mental representation of these permutations, to enter into the objective world of material stimuli and reactions. But Freud does not do this: he merely asserts that if it were done, then, probably, the loose ends would be tied up and energetics and the economic principle would be validated.

In conclusion, it must be noted that the economic viewpoint has been affixed *ab externo* to Freudian doctrine. He only alludes to it in passing, and it has no bearing upon the core of his doctrine. There is no truth in Bykhovskii's assertion that energetics is the fundamental foundation of psychoanalysis. Apparently, Bykhovskii is attaching to the term *energetics* the whole mental dynamic; and that is, of course, a rank absurdity. As for the mental dynamic, I have shown elsewhere that it is not at all a conflict of forces (in which energetics could find an application), but a conflict of vital ideological motives.

Finally, the dialectic.

I do not intend to dwell on this question to any great extent. All man's thinking is dialectical; man's subjective psyche, which is objectified in external and internal speech, is dialectical; myth and the delirium of the lunatic are dialectical. Furthermore, all manner of folly is dialectical; falsehood is dialectical; idle chatter and gossip fall, willy-nilly within the purview of the dialectic. (I remind the reader of the dialectic of gossip in Gogol', which determines the basic structure of his hyperbolic, grotesque style.) The dialectic is the very soul of all movement—even the movement of a fancy in the idle brain. It is really not surprising that even this picture of the vital ideological dynamic that Freud unfolds harbors an internal dialectic. But is this dialectic the same as the material dialectic of the natural world and history that is sought by the Marxist dialectical method?

Of course not! It is the dialectic of certain actual material forces, reflected in the mind, *ideologically refracted* and distorted. But Freud does not just uncover these material forces: he ignores their ideological—and hence secondary—nature, the particular refraction and distortion of his "mental dynamic," which is a dynamic of *motives*, not forces. There can be no talk of any materialist dialectic whatever in Freud's doctrine, since nothing in that doctrine ever goes beyond the bounds of the subjective psyche.

The overall shortcoming of Bykhovskii's article (a shortcoming that it shares with the other Freudian apologias still to be investigated) is its failure to approach the psychoanalytic method as an objective fact. It is necessary to take the method itself, in operation, and determine what it does and whither it is bound, instead of quoting random and contradictory pronouncements made by Freud and the Freudians about the method. A direct question ought to have been asked à propos of the free association method, to wit: What are the respective roles of introspection and objective observation in this method? The answer to such a directly and precisely posed question could hardly have occasioned any discomfiture. But Bykhovskii and the other apologists for Freudianism do not ask such direct questions of the method. They prefer instead to busy themselves marshaling quotations and declarative excerpts.

Here I shall end my examination of Bykhovskii's work. His thesis of Freudianism's *unconscious* reiteration of dialectical materialism remains unsubstantiated. This is one variant of the unconscious that does not, apparently, lend itself to being drawn into consciousness.

III

We pass now to A. R. Luria's work "Psychoanalysis as a system of monistic psychology."

This is Luria's view of Freudianism:

> Psychoanalysis, which shifted the theory of mental phenomena to an entirely new plane, the plane of the theory of organic processes taking place in the human organism as a whole, made a decisive break with the metaphysics and idealism of the old psychology, and has laid the first solid foundation (together with the theory of human responses and reflexes) . . . for a materialist, monistic psychology that takes a positive approach to the mind of the whole person.
> This is psychoanalysis's answer to the leading problem posed to modern psychology by the most important philosophy of the age, dialectical materialism, the problem of finding a materialist approach to the whole personality and the motive forces of the individual psyche.
> Psychoanalysis has made an important contribution to the resolution of this problem in that it has taken two major steps: *it has affirmed the interrelatedness of individual mental functions, and it has reintegrated the mind into the overall system of organs and their biologically determined activity.* (Pp. 79–80)

Freudianism is a psychology of the whole personality. In that assertion lies the crux of Luria's work.

As Luria sees it, the chief shortcoming of experimental psychology is the *mental atomism* that renders it incapable of approaching the person as an integral whole. He writes, "Since it was unable to undertake a scientific explanation of mental phenomena, experimental psychology took another route: it broke down its findings into discrete, minute elements, atomic facts, as it were, and studied each of these hypothetical elements of the mind separately" (p. 53).

Psychoanalysis is, in Luria's opinion, a reaction to this. "In contrast to scholastic, atomizing psychology, psychoanalysis starts out with the problems of the whole person; it proposes to study the person as a whole, and the processes and mechanisms that shape behavior" (p. 58).

Luria later demonstrates that study of the whole person is also the basic requirement of Marxist methodology, which approaches the individual as "an inseparable element of and an active force in history."

That is Luria's point of view.

One is compelled to agree with him that dialectical materialism does indeed require that the whole personality be studied, and provides the methodological foundations for such study (and is alone in so doing).

We know, however, that the idea of the "whole person" is certainly not exclusive to Marxism. And Marxism is not exactly preoccupied with spotlighting the "whole personality" and thrusting it into the foreground. We know that the idea of the whole personality was the culmination point of romantic idealism—of Schelling's philosophy of identity and of the teaching of Fichte. It was, in fine, the rallying cry of the romantic school. But the most consistent expression of the idea of the whole personality is found in the monadology of Leibniz. The monad is self-contained and sufficient unto itself, and at the same time reflects the entire world, appending the world to its internal unity. Could there be a more consistent incarnation of the idea of the whole personality? Moreover, it can be said that there is not—nor has there ever been—an antihistorical and antisocietal world view that has not advanced this same idea of the whole personality into the foreground.

Thus, this idea is a double-edged weapon that must be approached with special caution. Marxism has never spoken of the whole personality, or of any kind of personality, without making some specific and very important reservations. It utilizes such concepts in a highly dialectical manner.

The basic danger here is that [the idea of] the whole personality usually demands that a price be paid in *isolation and simplification*. The personality is defined in terms that isolate it and shut it off from the surrounding milieu. The personality is thus not an objective element of history, but a subjective unity, a self-sufficient center from which to experience the world. This "whole personality" is, of course, far more remote from Marxism than is the mental atomism of experimental psychology.

For Marxism, the requirement relating to the study of the whole personality is by no means a special, discrete requirement, as it is in individualism, in romanticism, or, for instance, in the contemporary differential (structural) psychology of William Stern and his school. No, it is simply part of Marxism's basic requirement that dialectical monism be brought to bear on study of the personality. The basic methodological requirement could be stated thus: the personality contains no absolutely isolated elements, since all is mutually interwoven, is merely part of the whole; nor is the personality itself isolated, since it, too, is merely part of the whole. Just as there are no isolated mental elements, so too there is no such thing as an isolated personality. The personality is whole (with respect to isolated elements); the personality is not whole (with respect to the life around it, of which it is an inseparable element). Both assertions are equally valid.

But this dialectical monism is attainable only under one condition—a pure, unadulteratedly objective approach to the personality. The personality should be understood and defined in the same terms as the material world around it. The Marxist formula for the personality and its conduct should include the same quantities as the formula for the societal, historical, and natural reality that surrounds it.

Does the Freudian psychology of the whole personality satisfy this condition? Not in the least!

The unconscious is even more adept than the consciousness of idealist psychology at isolating and enclosing the personality, at driving its life into the dead end of subjective-mental self-experience. The personality is allotted its own little history, its own little natural world, is broken into several internal personages (the ego, the ego-ideal, the id), and becomes a self-sufficient microcosm.

The arguments—or, rather, the quotations from Freud and the Freudians—with which Luria fills his paper cannot alter anything. One can concur with Luria's criticism of empirical psychology (the indictment of mental atomism). But what are the elements Freud uses to construct his whole personality? Those selfsame "atoms" of empirical psychology—notions, feelings, desires. The introduction of the unconscious has not changed a single thing. Broadly speaking, the concept of the "unconscious" is a great deal more subjectivist than the concept of "consciousness" in empirical psychology.

Does Freudianism really draw the mind into the system of the organism, as Luria would have us believe? Does it not, on the contrary, draw the material organism into the mental system?

The latter is, of course, the case. *In psychoanalysis, the organism is a secondary phenomenon.* It is an outright falsehood to represent the doctrine of erogenous zones as an objective physiological theory. According to this theory, the body is drawn into the personality's mental system, not vice versa. It is drawn, of course, not as an objective, external body, but as an experience of things corporeal, as an aggregate of internal instincts, desires, and notions. It is, so to speak, the body seen from the inside out.

The attempt to ascribe an objective character to the psychoanalytical concept of "drives" is also completely incorrect. Luria writes, ". . . for psychoanalysis, drives are not a purely psychological concept, but have a much broader sense, 'acting as a bridge between the mental and the somatic,' and are more of a biological nature."

No biologist would agree, of course, with such an odd definition of the biological as being a bridge between the soma and the psyche. Even Driesch, the vitalist, would disagree. There can, of course, be no talk of a concept that is a bridge between the subjectively mental and the objectively material, because experience offers no perspective from which such a unique hybrid may be descried. It is a purely metaphysical concept—one of the basic concepts of spiritualist metaphysics.

Thus, the psychoanalytic concept of the whole personality contains not one objective quantity that would make it possible for that personality to be incorporated into the surrounding material reality of the natural world. It is no easier to incorporate it into the objective socioeconomic process of history. We already know, after all, that Freud derives all objective, historical formations (the family, the tribe, the state, the church, and so forth) from those same subjectively mental roots, and that their existence begins and ends with that same interplay among internal subjective forces (power as the ego-ideal; societal solidarity as mutual identification, given the common nature of the ego-ideal; capitalism as the sublimation of anal eroticism, and so on).

Summing up, we can state that Freudianism, as a psychology of the whole personality, offers us a concept of the personality that serves to isolate and enclose—a concept of the way it subjectively experiences the world, not of its objective conduct in the world.

IV

In Fridman's work, which we shall now briefly examine, the center of gravity shifts to other facets of Freudianism. Here *the problem of ideology formation* comes to the fore.

The author expresses the Marxist viewpoint on ideology formation as follows: "Ideology is a system of inaccurate reflections of motives or sources of human activity" (p. 145). A little later, after presenting a quotation from Engels that endorses this point, the author continues:

> Since every kind of activity is performed by means of thought—since everything that excites a man to activity passes through his head—then thought is taken as the source of excitation. The error of "ideology" lies in the fact that it allows for the independence of thought ("consciousness") from other phenomena, which it then fails to research. The whole point is that the true, impelling forces, the prompting motives, remain beyond the ken of "ideology."

Fridman asserts that this Marxist perspective on ideology formation parallels Freud's view of it. He writes:

> From the viewpoint of Freud's doctrine, the provenance of "ideology" is in a rationalizing mechanism that is itself contingent on the process in which reasoning systems in general are formed. We have already pointed out, in describing this phenomenon, that its aim is to *conceal the true motives* of an aspiration under motives that are more elevated, more "ideal," and that originate, it would seem, in "consciousness." The fact that the personality remains oblivious of the real sources of these aspirations is explained by *the link between this process and the system* of the "unconscious." The formation of the "system," or the rationalizing procedure, is occasioned by a *need to avoid censure*, an importune tendency on the part of "consciousness" that explains why the need to justify it arises at all.

But, having come to an identical understanding of ideology formation, Marxism and Freudianism study diverse facets of this process, Fridman maintains, and thus complement each other splendidly. Marxism reveals the *source* of ideological phenomena, and Freudianism studies the actual *means*, the *mental mechanism* by which they are formed. "Historical materialism views the social 'consciousness' as a product and a reflection of the course of history—that is, of the conflict among varying 'desires' (interests) within society. Freud's doctrine provides an explanation of the process in which these desires are formed and the way in which their conflict is reflected in people's 'heads,' under the influence of external circumstances" (p. 152).

There is indeed a crude external similarity between the Marxist and the Freudian understanding of the mechanism of ideology formation. But it is a particular kind of similarity, reminiscent of the resemblance between a parody and its original.

In fact, ideology is a superstructure in Freudianism too, but upon what is that superstructure based? On the unconscious—that is, on displaced subjective instincts that are predominantly erotic. This is the psychoanalytic equivalent of the Marxist base! All the edifices of culture, according to Freud, tower over this peculiar base of displaced instincts. But, in addition to this, the Freudians hold that the actual Marxist base—the economy—is also a mere superstructure, raised upon that selfsame subjective base (a case in point is the Freudian definition of capitalism given above). The class struggle, which distorts ideologies, is the equivalent of the Freudian conflict between consciousness and the unconscious. Does this not smack of parody?

Psychoanalysis forces the actual mechanism of ideology formation into the narrow frame of the individual's subjective psyche, whereas in Marxism that mechanism is objective and societal. It presupposes the interaction of individuals within a collective that is organized on economic lines. Therefore, neither physiology nor psychology can reveal the complex objective process of ideology formation—and subjective psychology is the least competent of all in this. I have already had cause to mention that even the very simplest verbal utterance a man can make (a verbal reaction) cannot be confined within the individual organism

Furthermore, in Marxism the subjective psyche is certainly not the factor that distorts ideology. The correct, Marxist viewpoint is that not just the higher manifestations of consciousness but also all subjective-physical phenomena, everything that presents itself to man in the guise of internal experience, are ideological. The very language of his internal experience is ideological. The factors that distort ideology have a societal, class-based nature; they bear no trace of individual psychology. The hidden mainsprings of ideology—the objective socioeconomic forces—are located, of course, outside the ideologist's consciousness, but this does not mean that they are in his unconscious.

The very spirit of the Freudian doctrine of ideologies is profoundly inimical to Marxism. Freudianism is permeated by a typically uncouth, petit bourgeois yearning to expose the "elevated" and the "ideal" by reducing them to base "brutishness." The singular feature of Freudianism is that this base, brutish principle is represented as the all-powerful, extraspatial, timeless world of the unconscious—it is understood, that is, in a purely *spiritualist* manner. Freudianism is not alone here—note: *spiritualist nihilism* (or spiritualist cynicism) is a symptomatic phenomenon of the bourgeois here-and-now. There is more than a hint of nihilism inherent in Bergson's spiritualist doctrine of the *élan vital* (life force), which is hostile to reason and cultural forms, and also in his panegyrics to instinct. It is precisely this nihilist fascination for the exposé with a spiritualist foundation that has assured the success of Freudianism in petit bourgeois circles.

There is as much distance between this spiritualist nihilism and the Marxist understanding of the formula "Being defines consciousness" as there is between heaven and earth.

The Freudian mechanism of ideology formation (the same mechanism that, as we know, serves to form dreams and neurotic symptoms, according to Freud) is subjectivist, individualist, and spiritualist. It is a mechanism of isolated, self-sufficient, subjective experience of life—not at all the objective socioeconomic mechanism of the class struggle that, according to Marxist doctrine, determines the ideological refraction of existence in consciousness.

Fridman's thesis, which amounts to a claim that existence cannot determine consciousness without Freudian mechanisms, does not stand up under criticism.

V

It remains to examine the position of A. B. Zalkind. His viewpoint, which is no more than an attempt to provide Freudianism with a reflexological gloss, is fairly typical. There is no doubt as to the scientific value of reflexology for Marxism. There are, in fact, many who maintain that reflexology should be used as a touchstone to test the Marxist worth of any psychological theory.

A few words about reflexology are in order here. There is no gainsaying the immense scientific value of the reflexological method. However, this method's sphere of application is by no means as broad as some reflexologists would like it to be. It is a physiological method, a ramification of the one physiological method, and that is all. *The basic concepts of the reflexological method determine concrete experimental methodology*, and in this lie their significance and their value. Beyond reflexology's painstaking, infinitely slow, but reliable experimental method there is only vacuous *reflexological phrase-making*. The reflexological method is applied in an experiment—a new one each time—and that requires an enormous amount of time and effort. Though the method moves at a snail's pace, that pace is reliable. But when the basic reflexological concepts (the conditioned reflex, inhibition, etc.) are no longer used to organize experiments and become instead the organizing principle for what is almost a world view, when they are transferred with purely speculative ease to areas that are inaccessible to any kind of controlled experimental testing, those concepts forfeit all their scientific value. Marxism has nothing in common with this kind of reflexology.

Once detached from concrete experimental method, the apparatus of reflexological concepts turns into a platitudinous, vacuous schema that can be imposed upon quite literally anything. Why not conduct a reflexological exegesis of Kant's teaching, for example? The Kantian a priori is the unconditioned reflex reserve, conditioned reflexes are the a posteriori, and so forth—thus the reflexological validation of Kant. The absurdity of such an undertaking is clear to all. But I consider the work of translating any purely psychological theory into the language of reflexology not one whit more constructive or worthwhile.

But let us turn to Zalkind. How does he "reflexologize" Freudianism? What remains of Freudianism or of reflexology when two theories that stand at opposing ends of the methodological gamut are combined?

First of all, Zalkind rejects Freud's theory of sexuality.

"The majority," he writes (meaning the public at large), "is firmly convinced that the 'soul,' the peg, of Freudianism is his theory of sexuality, and that a critical attitude toward that theory constitutes a root-and-branch deathblow to all of Freudianism . . . In fact, however, the true center of the Freudianism that is radically agitating all of psychophysiology certainly does not rest in the theory of the sex instinct" ("Freudianism and Marxism," p. 165).

We should note first of all that Freud himself belongs to that majority, as do all orthodox and consistent Freudians. Freudianism deprived of its sexual "soul" is not altogether Freudianism.

Further, Zalkind enlists the reflexological method (applied phraseologically, not experimentally) to purify Freudianism of subjectivism and metaphysics.

"The reflexological method is our salvation. Its pure objectivism and biological monism demolish the metaphysical scaffolding around the edifice of Freudian doctrine and lay bare the sturdy materialist essence of real, undistorted Freudianism."

This is how Zalkind translates the Freudian pleasure principle into the language of reflexology:

> The pleasure principle should be understood as that portion of the physiological reserve that is connected with the minimal expenditure of energy by the organism—the portion that accumulates and reveals itself along the line of least internal resistance. It is, in other words, the organism's innate, inherited directives (unconditioned reflexes) and those strata of acquired, personal experience that developed directly and from the very outset from unconditioned reflexes, having required a minimal expenditure of effort for this purpose. The habits of childhood ("infantile" habits, according to Freud) are, of course, those formed early and most effortlessly, usually facilitated by every conceivable aid from significant adults (parents, siblings, etc.) and requiring no superfluous expenditure by the organism on concentration (the concentration reflex), orientation (the orientation reflex), and so forth. (P. 171)

The *displacement* mechanism is similarly "reflexologized." It is, of course, nothing other than *inhibition*.

> The psychoanalysts' basic concept, the one upon which they found all their subsequent structures—the concept of "displacement"—is reflexological. In the language of reflexes, it is termed "inhibition." The reflexive life of the organism consists in the revelation or the creation of certain reflexes and in the inhibition (displacement, dislodgement) or extinction of others. Reflexes, if one may so express it, compete among themselves; and one of them (or a group of them) is triumphant at the cost of dislodging (inhibiting) the rest—which victory is predicated upon an accumulation of maximum physical tension (Pavlov's focus of optimal excitation) around the former. The most advantageous reflex does not [always] triumph, of course. Where is the advantage of a canine food reflex that is coupled with an absurd auditory signal? But, in any event, one of them triumphs and becomes actual, moves into the lead, while the others are inhibited, dislodged. And psychoanalysts speak of this very thing. As the inhibiting influence of the stimuli that have dislodged the reflex weakens, the dislodged, displaced reflex

may, under the influence of any given new stimulus (irritant) appear, "break through," once again. Until then, though, it remains in a potential, inhibited state, overshadowed by the actual reflex field or, borrowing an old subjectivist term, overshadowed by consciousness, in the subconscious. And so for the time being, as we see, the psychoanalysts espouse concepts that are totally in keeping with the doctrine of conditioned reflexes. (A. B. Zalkind, *Suggestion and the life of the organism.* Gosizdat, 1927. P. 58)

Freud's intricate mechanism of dreams and suggestion (to the analysis of which he devotes several hundred pages) is so simplified by "reflexologization" that Zalkind's exposition literally takes up only three lines:

> The analysis of dream mechanisms and of the elements of suggestion is also given a reflexological interpretation.
> In sleep, when the action of external stimuli—which, as we have seen, all too often signify inhibition—ceases, that external calm itself becomes an inhibiting stimulus. (Article in *Krasnaia Nov'*, 1924, bk. 4, p. 175)

Once the basic Freudian mechanisms have been "reflexologized," the central concept of psychoanalysis—the concept of the unconscious—becomes, of course, entirely superfluous.

> And so the Freudian assertions that the subconscious has an independent existence, that it is isolated from the rest of the reflex reserve, that the subconscious is subject to a special kind of law, are found to be unsubstantiated. The "subconscious" of psychoanalysts turns out to be nothing more than a temporarily inhibited portion of the overall reflex reserve. There has been not the slightest deviation from reflexological doctrine. (*Suggestion and the life of the organism.* P. 59)

Having "reflexologized" Freudianism, Zalkind resorts to the arithmetic method of retroactive verification: he "Freudianizes" reflexology. (When applied to the dog, the Freudian mechanism looks most peculiar.)

> Exceedingly interesting in this sense are the experiments Pavlov's laboratory conducted with dogs (which the experimenters, of course, never even contemplated subjecting to a Freudian interpretation): by means of series of lengthy and assiduously organized stimuli (light, sound, or pain), the dog becomes incapable of reacting with his normal reflexes—seizing, salivating, and so on—to the aroma of the powdered meat that is brought to him, no matter how long it has been since he last ate, if the presentation of the powder is not accompanied by the appropriate conditioning "signals" (sound, light, etc.). At first there is persistent inhibition with respect to this new stimulus ("the protest of the pleasure principle")—the dog darts toward the powder, salivates, and so on—but the food is never given without the appropriate preliminary signals ("the reality principle"). Without "permission," without the conditioning signal, the dog is simply biochemically "unable" to eat (an absence of saliva and other secretions), has no "appetite," "does not want" to eat. (Article in *Krasnaia Nov'*, p. 173)

One may ask what remains of Freudianism after Zalkind has finished his job.

Freudianism without the category of the unconscious, without sexology, without the theory of instincts and, consequently, without the content of the unconscious; without the Oedipus complex, without the castration complex, and so on and so forth; without dream interpretation, without the ego and the id—in brief, Freudianism without Freudianism: such is the effect of "reflexologization."

What remains of the reflexological method?

Three platitudinous concepts; the unconditioned reflex, the conditioned reflex, inhibition—that is, the reflexological figures of speech remain, but no reflexology at all.

So—no Freudianism, and no reflexology!

The basic error of Zalkind's position is that it is not feasible to "reflexologize" another theory (as, in general, it is not feasible to translate any theory into the language of another theory). The reflexological method should be applied not to an alien theory, but to the fact, the material phenomenon—and application to fact implies that the study of that fact should be subordinated to a particular experimental method.

But do those facts of human behavior upon which Freudianism theorizes lend themselves at all to the reflexological method?

No, they do not. The reflexological method, being a purely physiological method, has power only over an abstractly identified component (a constituent part) of human behavior, but cannot provide an understanding of total behavior, which is not, after all, a mere physiological fact. I have already had occasion to mention this elsewhere (see Chapters VIII and IX). The conflicts of human behavior of which Freud speaks are not biological facts—they are objective sociological facts refracted through ideology. Zalkind's basic theoretical conviction that "the human psyche is a biological reflection of his sociological existence" (Article in *Krasnaia Nov'*, p. 163) therefore stands revealed as profoundly false. The entire subjective facet of the psyche— the facet that concerns Freud—is an *ideological* reflection of societal existence. The very phrase *biological reflection* strikes me as a profound philosophical absurdity. The basic thought in Zalkind's most recent book—which amounts to an attempt to gloss over the psychological factor in the life of the organism as an aggregate of conditioned reflexes—stands revealed as an out-and-out misconception.[2] Consciousness and the mental factor in general must be understood as *qualitatively unique*, and must not be reduced to conditioned reflexes. The mechanism of the conditioned reflex operates within the bounds of *an individual organism*, understood in the purely biological sense, and also of a purely *physical* milieu. When applied to man, that mechanism becomes an abstraction. Complex *socioeconomic* formations underlie the mind, and the mind itself needs a certain kind of *ideological* material—the word, the meaningful gesture, and so forth.

Only in this material does the subjective mind appear as an objective fact. Zalkind pays no heed to any of this.

The limits of this work do not permit me, of course, to go into more detail in my critical analysis of Zalkind's theory of the "mental factor" or in substantiating my view of the mind. I propose to do that elsewhere. The groundlessness of Zalkind's apologia for Freudianism has, I hope, been amply demonstrated.

VI

It remains to present my summation.

Psychoanalysis is a broad, organically unified doctrine that is deeply reasoned, according to its lights, and is indissolubly linked with the basic premises of the contemporary European bourgeoisie's class consciousness. Psychoanalysis is an intimate part of the decaying ideology of the bourgeoisie. We have seen that it is part and parcel of contemporary European thought. The Marxist apologists of Freudianism, in tackling the hopeless task of mixing oil and water, are obliged to destroy that organic unity (sick though the organism may be), to wrest from it individual elements and motifs, which change or lose their meaning once separated from the whole. Some of them, as we have seen, avoid objective analysis of the method itself and select individual declarative statements made by Freudians; others grasp at crude external similarities between individual features of Freudian theory and Marxism; and others, such as Zalkind, replace Freudianism with an abridged form of reflexology.

A calm, objective analysis of all facets of Freudianism can surely leave no doubt whatever as to the legitimacy of the Marxist assessment of that doctrine presented here.

Notes

1. Bykhovskii knows this perfectly well. Elsewhere in this paper he says: "Awareness of the unconscious—such is the motto of psychoanalytical therapy." How can this be reconciled with the statements cited here?

2. See Chapter IX of Zalkind's book *Suggestion and the life of the organism*, "The psychological factor in the light of the doctrine on reflexes," pp. 48–72.

V. N. Voloshinov and the Basic Assumptions
of *Freudianism* and Structuralism

Neal H. Bruss

In Voloshinov's *Freudianism*, emergent structuralism judged youthful psycho-analysis. Their meeting would have been significant enough if the two disciplines only had grown to prominence as human sciences, and all the more significant if Voloshinov had been only moderately insightful about psychoanalysis.

Voloshinov raised what would become fundamental questions in psychoanalysis to the present day: Is psychoanalysis entitled to a deterministic instinctual framework or only a framework of human actions (Schafer 1976)? Would an instinctual frame-work qualify psychoanalysis as a natural science (Hartmann 1964)? Is there "mean-ingful" experience before language acquisition (Waelder 1937; Meissner 1980)? Are there non-subjective validators of psychoanalytic interpretations (Edelson 1984)?

Voloshinov's approach to psychoanalysis turned on basic assumptions of both disciplines—the sign's establishment on social convention for structuralism, and the reality of the unconscious for psychoanalysis. The philosophical perspective of even early structuralism may have given Voloshinov a critical perspective not available within psychoanalysis itself. But any response to his criticisms from psychoanalysis clarifies fundamental issues in structuralism as well. Such a response can be made based on works by Freud which Voloshinov mentioned.

Psychical Continuity and the Unconscious

Voloshinov took the core of psychoanalysis to be the concept of the unconscious, which he criticized as a deterministic, individualistic fiction. He argued that the un-conscious had no material reality, but served psychoanalysis's true function—as one more decadent European ideology of the preeminence of the sexual instincts and denial of the essentiality of social life.

Psychoanalysis would reply that the unconscious derived from inferences based on a "basic assumption" that Voloshinov did not discuss. This basic assumption is of "psychical continuity": that a person's experience is continuous, and therefore that gaps in memory, or seemingly inexplicable or conflicted behavior must be explained—"interpreted"—in relation to the rest of the continuity.

The *locus classicus* for this basic assumption is Freud's definition of the meaningfulness of the symptom in the *Introductory Lectures on Psycho-Analysis* as "the intention it serves and its place in a psychical continuity" (1916–17: 40; repeated p. 61; see Bruss 1986).

Thus, when Voloshinov emphasized "the unconscious," he took one, static part of a dynamic for the whole. What was dynamic was the passage of the contents of the psychical continuity from one "system" or modality of consciousness to another. Freud stated in *The Interpretation of Dreams*:

> The unconscious wishful impulses clearly try to make themselves effective in daytime as well [as in dreams], and the fact of transference [of infantile relations to the therapist], as well as the psychoses, show us that they endeavor to force their way by way of the preconscious system into consciousness and to obtain the power of movement. Thus the censorship between the *Ucs.* and the *Pcs.*, the assumption of whose existence is positively forced upon us by dreams, deserves to be recognized and respected as the watchman of our mental health. [1900:567]

Psychoanalysis would therefore respond that the unconscious is not more appropriately understood as the center of psychoanalysis than the preconscious—perhaps less so, in that the preconscious is the seat of judgment as to what passes into consciousness.

Voloshinov would have seized upon the notion of a static unconscious because of his constant emphasis in *Freudianism* on language, and all human expression, as "determined in all the fundamentals and essentials of its content by objective-social factors" (p. 86). Such a view has no need for psychical dynamism if it takes human expression as already "determined" by social factors at the moment of expression.

Introspection and Science

Under Freud's theory, thoughts only become conscious if they satisfy preconscious censorship. Traumatic thoughts repressed into the unconscious only reach consciousness and gain partial expression in thought, language, or behavior after having undergone defensive distortion. They are represented as compromise-formations, symptoms—the *Interpretation of Dreams* was Freud's principal demonstration that the modes of distortion were systematic and could be reversed inferentially with the supplemental material of patients' free associations on those symptoms. But Voloshinov writes as though psychoanalysis took patients' associations literally, as veridical introspections. Further, Voloshinov felt that psychoanalysis's claim to scientific status failed if after all its metapsychology psychoanalysis relied on such wholly subjective material.

Voloshinov quoted Freud's important statement in *The Ego and the Id*, "We come to know the unconscious only by making it conscious" (1923: 19; quoted above, p. 49). He then concluded, "Freud's construct remains within the confines of what a person himself can say about himself and his behavior on the basis of his own internal apprehension" (p. 77). He seems not to have recognized that Freud assumed that "what a person himself can say about himself" is *itself* distorted, and the person's "internal apprehension" censored. Or, that psychoanalysis understood patients' free associations as symptomatic: as products of distortion needful of interpretation.

Voloshinov may have overestimated psychoanalysis's trust in introspection because his concept of the social determination of human expression did not entail psychical dynamism, in this case, the distortion of thought by one psychical agency before it permitted the thought to enter another agency.

But Voloshinov did make an effort to account for the psychoanalytic insight on intrapsychic conflict—by re-locating the conflict in the "determining" social reality.

Symptomatic Expression, Conflict, and Language

Voloshinov accepted Freud's analysis that conflict was expressed in symptoms such as "dreams, myth, witticism, and all the verbal components of the pathological formations" (p. 88). But Voloshinov suggested explaining these expressions with a concept of "behavioral ideology," which he based on inner speech "at a great distance from the stable system of the ruling ideology":

> that inner and outward speech that permeates our behavior in all its aspects . . . more
> sensitive, more responsive, more excitable and livelier than an ideology that has under-
> gone formulation and become "official" . . . . [in which] accumulate those contradic-
> tions which, once having reached a certain threshold, ultimately burst asunder the sys-
> tem of the official ideology . . . but related just as much to the socioeconomic basis and
> is subject to the same laws of development as ideological superstructures in the proper
> sense of the term. [p. 88]

Voloshinov's explanation of psychical conflict as *social* conflict, thus, turns on language. But Voloshinov defined language in terms of the social: "*The verbal component of behavior is determined in all the fundamentals and essentials of its content by objective-social factors*" (p. 86). His explanation is therefore circular. Further, without some agency to mediate language and ideology, individuals and societies, let alone inner and outer speech, Voloshinov's alternative cannot explain how persons recognize and address conflict—as inner speech or in any other form.

The emphasis on language as social product is fundamental to structuralism, evocative of Saussure's remark about language as social convention: that the signifier "is fixed, not free, with respect to the linguistic community that uses it . . . for language furnishes the best proof that a law accepted by a community is a thing that is tolerated and not a rule to which all freely consent" (p. 70).

Structuralism—Voloshinov's, Saussure's, or any other's—is liable to difficulty in accounting for conflict and its consequences, whether in language acquisition, style-shifting, or historic change, in that the assumption of conventionality does not entail un- or anti-conventionality: communicative chaos, not opposition, would have been the case before the social convention. Its basic assumption confines it to recapitulating the mythic social convention: correlating linguistic forms with social-contextual features of one sort or another, whether of the purely linguistic context, the situation of use or the demographics of the users.

The psychoanalytic assumption of the intentionality of all expressive behavior empowers it to correlate values—personal and social—of signs. It can therefore induce the place of a conflict in an individual's experience, reconstructing the forces in conflict and the psychical values associated with them by the subject. The assumption of intentionality does not make a human science vulnerable to a mentalistic "intentional fallacy" of *ad hoc* attribution of *particular* motives, the validity claims for a psychoanalytic reconstruction of a gap or contradiction in a psychical continuity are bound by the constraints on inductive arguments in general, and supported by the weight of individual and case study evidence in the discipline (Edelson 1984).

Family as First Society in Psychoanalysis

Conceding to Voloshinov that language has a social life and that socioeconomic forces affect individuals, psychoanalysis would draw attention to the abstractness of Voloshinov's theoretical references to "the social" and the lack of attention to the *concrete* social structures central to psychoanalysis: the family and the peer group. Rather than accepting itself characterized as "asocial," psychoanalysis could argue that is has always argued that psychical development is *necessarily* inter-personal or "social," in that humans only develop among other people, typically the family.

Freud stated the psychoanalytic developmental theory in a work which Voloshinov mentioned, *Three Essays on the Theory of Sexuality* (1905b). He argued that in resolving the Oedipal conflict, the family teaches the child to modulate his or her instincts in terms, first, of their wishes and, second, of the language and customs of the larger society in which the family lives. In theoretical terms, the child develops a psychical agency for coping with reality, an ego, on the examples of the older people who raise him. When forced with the demand to relinquish gratification, the child "internalizes" the parents' demands, consigning a part of his ego to represent them as a conscience, or superego.

The child fears that his willfulness will result in being abandoned or punished by the adults whom he loves and on whom he is dependent. He resolves his fear by accepting their strictures as his own, remaking a part of himself in their stern image. (This psychoanalytic hypothesis of the formation of conscience follows from the assumption of the psychical continuity through observations of children before, during, and after heightened conflict with parents and expression of versions of their values; it leaves psychoanalysis with the continuing task of explaining "internalization," "identification," and "introjection" of the parents' psychical attributes [Meissner 1981].)

This remaking is necessarily partial, in that one aspect of the child presides over remaking itself, judging the child's own instincts and avowing the adults' strictures. For psychoanalysis, such a primal split is a necessary condition of becoming a human being. But it is also a source of conflict to the extent that the particular adult models acquired by the child leave instinctual drives unappeased and the growing child is unprepared to manage them as demands.

Psychoanalysis observes directly in children and, reconstructively, in adult patients, that the "resolution" of the conflict with parents over control of the instincts is so great a blow to childish self-esteem that it is repressed from consciousness. Further, after compromising so greatly, the child turns somewhat from his or her parents to peers. But the structures developed by children in the setting of the family are persistent because they are *formative* of the person. Hence, even when the child turns toward peers, the family's will (and the child's accommodation to it) endures— as an important part of the child's psychical structure: conscience. The child thus can only repeat ways of mediating experience learned from the family. For psychoanalysis, then, the social role of the family is undeniable, and essential.

That individuals respond to new acquaintances, including and especially the psychotherapist, with their patterns of response to members of their family is a psychoanalytic conclusion based on observation and the assumption of psychical continuity. Psychoanalysis does not argue, as Voloshinov suggests, that repetition constitutes the totality of patient-analyst relations, but rather that repetition is inevitable, and as a type of symptom, is the central material of interpretation and treatment. Nor does psychoanalysis assert that the patient responds to the analyst *exactly* like a parent, but rather that the transference is also heavily qualified by, among other things, the therapeutic situation and general resistance against the return of repressed material.

The Oedipal resolution, the child's relinquishment of infantile pleasures and acceptance of family norms under threat, is so important developmentally and so prone to difficulty that psychoanalysis can define its object of study as the passage from human animal infancy to personhood and its vicissitudes. If transference symptoms repeat that passage, they must be critically important data for psychoanalysis.

Group Psychology and the Analysis of the Ego (1921) analyzed the transference in peer and group relations in such organizations as the tribe, the church, and the army. Such interpretations follow from the basic assumption, that behavior in those groups is *continuous* with behavior in the family.

Instinct

But Voloshinov does mention the family, at least when referring to sexuality as "the supreme criterion of *reality*" for psychoanalysis and accusing psychoanalysis of "*the wholesale sexualization of the family . . . that castle and keep of capitalism*" (p. 90–91).

Voloshinov reads psychoanalysis as a decadent European philosophy like Bergsonism, Nietzscheism and Spenglerism, a "popular ideological trend," a "modest

psychiatric method" which had elaborated "a general theory of psychology," including a "philosophy of culture" (p. 7). Voloshinov named "instinctual determinism" as
its "basic ideological motif"—that "a person's consciousness is shaped not by his
historical existence but by his biological being, the main facet of which is sexuality"
(pp. 9–10). For Voloshinov, the dominant feature of the ideology is "the strife, the
chaos, the adversity" (p. 75), "the conflict of [purportedly] elemental forces" (p. 76),
"the leitmotif of crisis and decline," the ignorance of the social nature of human beings espoused by a social class "find[ing] itself in a state of disintegration . . . compelled to retreat from the arena of history" (pp. 10–11). Psychoanalysis expressed a
"distrust of consciousness" and "a fear of history" (pp. 13–14), "no room is left for
the reflection of objective socioeconomic existence, with its forces and conflicts"
(p. 60).

The concordance to Freud's Standard Edition by Samuel Guttman et al. (1980)
indicates that Freud mentioned Nietzsche 15 times and Bergson, 8, but Spengler, 0.
Freud discussed these philosophers, as Voloshinov said, as agreeing with him about
one aspect or another of human instinct. But Freud's interest in these philosophers
should be understood in the context of his interest in creative writers: he believed,
simply, that artists anticipated many of his observations. The concordance also reveals that Freud mentioned Goethe 110 times and Shakespeare 60 times, but the
philosophers Socrates or Plato only a total of 17 times, and Hegel twice.

Freud's "instinctual determinism" and "philosophy of culture" must also be understood in light of Freud's admiration for Darwin (34 mentions in the Standard Edition).
Freud seemed to feel that psychoanalysis required an evolutionary component. Citing Darwin, Freud argued that the species had passed through the same stages of
psychical development as an individual: he attributed the hypothetical universal
symbolism associated with his student C. G. Jung to physical "traces" left behind of
the development of the species. Freud readily acknowledged his debt to Darwin but
only notes his concurrence with, say, Nietzsche.

Darwin's The Expression of Emotions in Man and Animals was the closest of Darwin's work to the bases of psychoanalysis, for it explored the transitional area between feeling and language. Freud invoked it explicitly in his contribution to the
Studies on Hysteria, arguing that language developed from the expression of intense
emotion, and, conversely, that the language of modern humans had lost much of the
urgency of archaic emotional life (Freud and Breuer 1893–95:181).

Freud argued that crying was the precursor of communication in infants, in that,
although it initially released the infant's tension, it also communicated need and
summoned help from adults. Freud thus posited an evolutionary motive for language. The structuralist basic assumption, that language is established by social convention, is not the consequence of the search for such a motive—the need to explain
why human beings needed such conventions on meaning in the first place. The instincts whose theoretical role Voloshinov condemns thus provided psychoanalysis
with the motive for language, which, in turn, Voloshinov treats as central to social

life. Psychoanalysis would respond that the burden is on Voloshinov to name some other motive for language.

Discussing "Oedipal theory," Voloshinov accepts as "facts" the instinctual behavior on which the psychoanalytic developmental theory is based, but to him they seem insignificant:

> What would remain, then? A number of piecemeal objective observations that can be made about the behavior of a child: the early excitability of the sexual organs (e.g., infant erection) and of other erogenous zones, the difficulty of weaning a child away from his constant closeness to his mother's body (particularly, of course, the breast), and so on. There is obviously no need to contest a set of facts of this sort—they are commonly accepted facts. [p. 81]

These "objective observations" would be enough for psychoanalysis, because they establish the motive for language and culture—in the dependent human mammal's need to achieve relief from instinctual domination among other humans who can help him.

Early Experience

Voloshinov used Otto Rank's *The Trauma of Birth* as "a magnificent *reductio ad absurdum*" (p. 64) of the Freudian attribution of all experience to instinctual development. He claimed that "under no circumstances can it [Rank's book] be claimed as a mere eccentricity. It expressed the full spirit of Freudianism today" (p. 62).

Voloshinov could not know that Rank and his sympathizers were referred to as "the birth brigade" by students and colleagues of Freud such as his editor-translators James and Alix Strachey, who, in the words of their own editors, provide "the story of [Rank's] gradual expulsion from the psychoanalytic fold in their later letters." (Strachey and Strachey [1985] : 108).

The central psychoanalytic position was that psychical development was only possible with the readiness for thought and language which would free the infant partially from the dominion of his instincts and initiate him into family and social life. For psychoanalysis to accept the psychical consequentiality of the "birth trauma" would conflict with its position that psychical development required and co-occurred with language acquisition.

Psychoanalysis tied language to psychical development in much the same way that Voloshinov tied "inner speech" to ideology: in both, the linguistic ordering of experience reflects an endless process by which new humans are produced. This tie to language makes the similarity between Voloshinov and Freud seem as important as their differences, the shared emphasis on the linguistic foundation of personhood in an ongoing human world essential, the difference between "social" and "psychological" only a matter of terminological emphasis, although Voloshinov could hardly have been expected to recognize this.

Moreover, one sign of the underlying agreement of Voloshinov and Freud on the matter of language and psychical development is that Voloshinov's isolation of Rank for criticism anticipates the reaction of the central Freudians to a later claim for prelinguistic experience. Melanie Klein and her students attributed to infancy a primitive psychical mechanism, "projective identification," functioning before language acquisition, which they find operating regressively in some of the most extreme forms of adult disturbance. The Kleinian argument was more sophisticated than Rank's in that the primitive psychical mechanism, with which an angry infant "projects" pain and other "bad self-parts" into the mother or other external object, was claimed to be a precondition for language development. The mechanism is considered "primitive" because, in opposition to the Freudian mechanisms of symptom-formation which postdate language acquisition, "projective identification" is ignorant of boundaries and differences between ordinary objects and persons. But Klein's critics have emphasized the same criticism that Voloshinov made against Rank, that an infant is incapable of even a primitive psychical mechanism before language acquisition (Bruss 1986).

Transference

Voloshinov criticized the transference theory as a false "emphasis on individual psyche" of a "complex *social interrelationship* between doctor and patient" (pp. 78–79). For Voloshinov, what psychoanalysis called conflict between conscious and unconscious "are only possible between two ideas, two ideological trends or two antagonistic persons, and not between two natural material forces . . . *not a dynamic of psychical forces but only a dynamic of various motives of consciousness*" (p. 77). An objective psychologist, as opposed to a psychoanalyst, "does not take verbal utterances on trust—or any motivation or explanation that a person himself, on the basis of his own inner apprehension, might give his behavior" (p. 78). Psychoanalysis could respond that, in any case, its interest in transference phenomena is not where Voloshinov placed it, on the individual-social issue, but on the matter of *repetition* of patterns set by early structuration.

Nonetheless, in what was probably the most extreme adjustment of his career, Freud protected the social-interactional emphasis when he neutralized the doctor's countertransference onto the patient with the requirement of a training analysis. Voloshinov wrote, "Freud's system projects the entire dynamics of the interrelationship between two people into the individual psyche" (p. 80). At one point, when the method of symptom-interpretation was just emerging, Freud did place the emphasis of psychotherapy on the interpretation of the *textual* nature of the patient's symptoms at the cost of inattention to the patient-therapist interaction—what Voloshinov called "conflict . . . between two persons."

Voloshinov divided Freud's work into three periods. The first period was based on his work with Joseph Breuer, the *Studies on Hysteria.* The second period was "dry and business-like," with "an emphatically positivistic character," in which were written "all of Freud's basic psychoanalytic works": *The Interpretation of Dreams*, *Jokes and Their Relation to the Unconscious*, *Three Essays on the Theory of Sexuality*, and the *Introductory Lectures*.

In the third period, contemporaneous with Voloshinov's critique, the works of Freud's newer followers emerged, and like them, Freud "ha[d] begun to approach . . . metaphysical doctrines. . . . *General issues of Weltanschauung now begin to take precedence over particular, specialized problems*." Voloshinov counts in this period *Beyond the Pleasure Principle* and *The Ego and the Id*—and Otto Rank's *The Trauma of Birth*. (He also makes reference to *Group Psychology and the Analysis of the Ego*.)

But another set of events concerning language might be used to define these periods of Freud's writing. The "basic psychoanalytic works" of the second period establish the method of interpretation which allowed Freud to interpret symptoms as texts: condensation, displacement, negation, overdetermination, symbolization, secondary revision. Without this interpretive armamentarium, in the *Studies on Hysteria*, Freud relied on the basic principle of logic-by-association to interpret his patients' symptoms, and his case studies are written quite close to his patients' experience. The emphasis in the major case studies, published shortly after the major second period interpretive works, is on the interpretation of the symptoms, rather than the encounter with the patients.

In particular, *Fragment of an Analysis of a Case of Hysteria* (1905a), the first of the case studies, focused on Freud's interpretation of his patient Dora's two dreams—and on her resistance to receiving his interpretations. Freud is in combat with Dora as he is not with any of the patients discussed in the *Studies* or any thereafter.

In the afterword to the case study, Freud admitted having underestimated Dora's transference, the projection onto himself of traits of her father, while interpreting her dreams to her. From then on, he balanced his first-period work on interpretive method by emphasis on the here-and-now of patients' symptoms in therapy.

Freud had to free psychoanalysis from the emphasis on textuality of symptoms that accrued from the discovery of the interpretive method and return to it the emphasis on interaction. Voloshinov discussed transference largely as repetitions of past relationships, missing its effect of anchoring the psychoanalysis in the here-and-now of the patient's behavior. Thus Freud had to achieve the "complex social situation" (p. 79), the interpersonal element that Voloshinov found lacking.

Overdetermination

The differences in emphasis which follow from the differences in content of the basic assumptions held by Voloshinov and Freud reveal themselves, finally, in different senses of causality held by them. Voloshinov, for example, criticized Freudianism for arguing that "all ideological creativity . . . springs from . . . psycho-organic roots" (p. 57). "No room is left for the reflection of objective socioeconomic existence with its forces and conflicts."

Psychoanalysis might respond that it holds a different view of "determination" than Voloshinov, that it takes symptomatic expression as "overdetermined," a term which first appeared in the *Studies on Hysteria* (Freud and Breuer 1893–95:212).

In the *Studies*, Freud and Breuer argued that hysterical symptoms were "returns" of repressed traumas, and that therefore a symptom was an unsuccessful defense against repetition of a trauma. They added that in some cases, the earlier traumas were multiple, that the symptom summed multiple traumas. In *The Interpretation of Dreams*, Freud argued that every dream embodied both the preceding day's residues, including objective socioeconomic existence with its forces and conflicts, and a repressed infantile wish, and that preconscious censorship composed dreams from such materials. In *Three Essays*, he argued that the psychical structures, id, ego, and superego, contributed to dreams. In *Group Psychology and the Analysis of the Ego*, he argued that psychical evolution left traces which were expressed in symptoms as symbolism.

For psychoanalysis, a symptom can be expected to express more than one meaning. Overdetermination of meaning, then, follows from the assumption of psychical continuity—that symptomatic expressions are found to be determined by several points in a person's experience. Nothing in the assumption of a social convention itself leads to "overdetermination," although by examining actual language, structuralist successors of Voloshinov have arrived at variants of the concept. The Czech "functional sentence perspective" theorists (Daneš 1964) and the British functional linguistics of M. A. K. Halliday (1973) see every utterance achieving basic textual, semantic, and social ends; Labov's (1972a and b) concept of variable rules takes level of formality of an utterance to be determined by socioeconomic features of context and the identities of the interlocutors, as well as by linguistic factors. The interest in symptomatic expression that brought Voloshinov to criticize Freud's explanation of its determination could lead structuralism to recognize Freud's insight on multiple meaning.

References

Bruss, Neal H. (1986). Validation in psychoanalysis, and projective identification. *Semiotica*, 60 (1/2), 129–192.

Daneš, F. (1964). A three-level approach to syntax. In *Travaux Linguistiques de Prague I*. Prague: Editions de l'Académie Tchechoslovaque des Sciences.

Edelson, Marshall (1984). *Hypothesis and Evidence in Psychoanalysis*. Chicago and London: University of Chicago Press.

Freud, Sigmund (1900). *The Interpretation of Dreams*, trans. James Strachey. (*The Standard Edition of the Complete Psychological Works* [hereafter, *Standard Edition*] 4 and 5, James Strachey, gen. ed.). London: Hogarth Press and the Institute of Psycho-Analysis.

——— (1905a). Fragment of an analysis of a case of hysteria [the Dora case], trans. Alix Strachey and James Strachey. *Standard Edition* 7, 1–122.

——— (1905b). *Three Essays on the Theory of Sexuality*, trans. James Strachey. *Standard Edition* 7, 123–245.

——— (1915–16). *Introductory Lectures on Psycho-Analysis*, trans. James Strachey. *Standard Edition* 15 [p. 239] and 16.

———— (1921). *Group Psychology and the Analysis of the Ego,* trans. James Strachey. *Standard Edition* 18, 65–143.

———— (1923). *The Ego and the Id,* trans. Joan Riviere. *Standard Edition* 19, 1–66.

————, and Breuer, Joseph (1893–1895). *Studies on Hysteria,* trans. James Strachey and Alix Strachey. *Standard Edition* 2.

Guttman, Samuel A., Jones, Randall L., and Parrish, Stephen M. (1980). *The Concordance to The Standard Edition of the Complete Psychological Works of Sigmund Freud.* Boston: G. T. Hall.

Halliday, M. A. K. (1973). *Explorations in the Functions of Language.* New York: Oxford University Press, and Amsterdam: Elsevier.

Hartmann, Heinz (1964). *Essays on Ego Psychology, Selected Problems in Psychoanalytic Theory.* New York: International Universities Press.

Labov, William (1972a). *Language in the Inner City: Studies in the Black English Vernacular.* Philadelphia: University of Pennsylvania.

Labov, William (1972b). *Sociolinguistic Patterns.* Philadelphia: University of Pennsylvania.

Meissner, W. W. (1980). A note on projective identification. *Journal of the American Psychoanalytic Association* 28 (1), 43–67.

Meissner, W. W. (1981). *Internatalization in Psychoanalysis* (Psychological Issues monograph 50). New York: International Universities Press.

Saussure, Ferdinand de (1959). *Course in General Linguistics,* trans. Wade Baskin, Charles Bally, Albert Sechehaye, and Albert Reidlinger (eds.). New York, Toronto, and London: McGraw-Hill.

Schafer, Roy (1976). *A New Language for Psycho-analysis.* New Haven and London: Yale.

Strachey, James, and Strachey, Alix (1985). *Bloomsbury/Freud: The Letters of James and Alix Strachey, 1924–1925,* Perry Meisel and Walter Kendrick (eds.). New York: Basic Books.

Waelder, Robert (1937). The problem of the genesis of psychical conflict in earliest infancy. *International Journal of Psycho-Analysis* 18(4): 406 73.

INDEX

Annenskij, I., 113
Art, 3, 5, 7, 58, 59–60, 87, 94–96. See
  also Literature/verbal art
  as social communication, 97
Artistic form, 107–109, 113–15
  and content, 108–109

Barbier, A., 113
Baxtin (Bakhtin), M. M., xii, xv–xix,
  xxi–xxiii, xxiv n.8, xxv n.19
Baxtin (Bakhtin) Circle, x–xi, xii–xiii, xvi
Behaviorism, 18, 23, 68
Bergson, H., 8, 12–13, 14, 73, 91, 127,
  137, 138
Bernheim, H., 30, 32, 85
Bexterev, V., 18
"Beyond the Social" (Vološinov), xix–xxi
Biology (Biologism), 11–15, 45, 72–73, 91,
  125, 131
Blonskij, P., 18
Bourgeoisie, vii, ix, 8–9, 79, 87, 89–91,
  115, 127, 132
  philosophy of, 11–12, 14
Breuer, J., 7, 30, 33, 34, 140, 142
Bykhovskii, B., 118–23

Capitalism, viii, 90, 115, 137
Castration complex, 59
Catharsis/cathartic method, 33, 34
Censorship, 37, 44, 46, 49, 51, 70, 77, 89,
  134
Charcot, J., 29, 30
Class consciousness, 25–26, 77, 132
  and self-consciousness, 87
Class struggle, xi, xii, 25, 127
Compromise/compromise formations,
  49–51, 54–55, 56, 134
Confession, 34
Conflict of psychical forces/motives, 76, 77,
  78, 83, 85, 88, 137, 140. See also Dy-
  namics of the psyche
Conscious, the/consciousness, viii, ix, xi,
  xiii, xx, 10, 12, 13, 24, 29–30, 32–33,
  34, 37, 41, 42–43, 44–46, 48, 49,
  50–52, 68–69, 76–77, 85–87, 89, 119,
  125, 126–27, 134–35, 137, 138, 140
Conventionality, 136

Danës, F., 142
Darwin, C., 76, 138
Death instinct, 45, 76, 121
Dewey, J., 18
Dialectical materialism, xxii, 21, 22, 83,
  118, 122–23, 124
Displacement, 129
Dostoevskij, F., xv, xxi, 59, 112–13
Dreams, analysis of, 50–55, 130, 142
Driesch, H., xxv n.19, 12, 14, 125
Dynamics of the psyche/psychical dynamics,
  vii–ix, x, 35, 37, 56, 75–83, 86, 134,
  135–36, 140

Ego, 46, 48, 61, 78
Ego instinct, 39, 44, 73, 76, 78, 121
Energetics, 120–22
Engels, F., vii, 126
Entelechy, 14
Enthymeme, 100–101
Ermakov, I., 59
Erogenous zones, 40–41, 71–72, 81
Eros, 45, 76, 121
Experiment, psychological, 19–21
Experimental psychology, 18, 19, 123
External/objective apprehension, 20, 21, 22,
  69
  versus internal/subjective apprehension,
  18–19, 72

Family, 136–37
Ferenczi, S., 31, 43
Fichte, J., 12, 124
Forgetting, 55–56
Formalism, 91, 96, 107, 116
Free association, 35, 50, 54, 85, 119, 122,
  134–35
Freud, S., viii, ix, xi–xii, xix–xx, 7–10, 17,
  22, 24, 29, 30–33, 34, 39–42, 44–46,
  48, 49–50, 52, 54–55, 67–73, 76–78,
  85, 119, 120–22, 125, 126, 129, 130,
  131, 133, 134, 138, 139–42
  Ego and the Id, The, 46–47, 134–35
  Group Psychology and the Analysis of the
    Ego, 60–61, 137
  Interpretation of Dreams, 50–55, 134,
    141, 142

Jokes and Their Relation to the Uncon-
   scious, 58–59, 141
Psychopathology of Everyday Life, 55–56
Studies on Hysteria (with Breuer), 7, 30,
   138, 140, 141, 142
Three Essays on the Theory of Sexuality,
   40–41, 136, 141
Freudianism, xx–xxi, 117–32. *See also*
   Psychoanalysis
   ideological motif of, 14
   as ideological trend, 8–11, 13, 64, 89, 91
   philosophy of culture of, 7, 57, 62. *See*
   also Art; Myths; Religion; Social forms
   psychological theory of, 17, 24–25, 30,
   41, 67–72, 75–78, 82–83, 85
Fridman, B. D., 118, 126–28

Gesture, 104
Glasnost', xxiv n.8
Glück, H., xvii
Goethe, J., 138
Gogol', N., 59, 122
Gomperz, N., 12, 13
Grammar, 110–11
Groddeck, G., 72, 120

Halliday, M. A. K., 142
Hartmann, E., 30, 31
Hegel, G. F. W., 12, 138
Heine, H., 113
Holquist, M., xvii, xxv n.19
Hypnoid, 34
Hypnosis, 7, 32, 34, 61
Hysteria, 33–34, 142

Id, 46, 59, 61, 76, 78
Idealization, 60–61
Identification, 47, 60
Ideological/cultural creativity, 50, 57, 61,
   62–63
Ideology, 77, 85–86, 87–88, 89, 90, 95,
   98, 126–28
   behavioral, 88–89, 133, 135, 137–38,
   139
   official and unofficial, 89–90
   revolutionary, 90
Individualism, 78, 80, 87
   in aesthetics, 97–98, 108
Inhibition, 129–30
Inner speech, x–xi, xxi, 21, 23–24, 114,
   139
   and outward speech, xii, xxi, 79, 86, 89,
   114–16, 135
Instinct, 12, 39, 44, 45, 72–73, 121–22,
   133, 137–39. *See also* Death instinct; Ego
   instinct; Sexual instinct
Intentionality, 136

Internal/subjective apprehension, 17, 73,
   78, 83. *See also* External/objective
   apprehension
Intonation, 102–105, 106, 108, 111
Intrauterine state, 52, 62–64
Introspection/self observation, 19–20, 77,
   81, 134–35
Ivanov, V. V., xvi

Jakobson, R., xv, xvii
James, W., 13, 18, 80
Jameson, F., xvii
Janet, P., 30
Jokes, 58–59
Jung, C., 138
Juvenal, 113

Kant, E., xxii, 12, 13, 69
Klein, M., 140
Konkin, S. S., xxiv n.8
Kornilov, K., 18

Labov, W., 142
Laforgue, J., 113
Language, social/ideological nature of, x, xx,
   xxi, 22, 79, 83, 86–88, 99–100, 105,
   106, 133, 134, 135–36, 138–40, 141,
   142. *See also* Verbal discourse; Verbal
   utterance
Language and linguistics, 79, 83, 106, 109,
   110, 116
Leibniz, G., 124
Lenin, V., vii
Libido. *See* Sexual instinct
Lièbault, A., 30
Lipps, T., 29
Literature/verbal art, 79, 93–94, 106–16
Loeb, J., xx–xxi, 83
Luria, A. R., 118, 123–25
Lyric, the, 113

"Making strange," 91
Marxism, xvii–xviii, xix–xxi, xxii–xxiii, 17,
   21, 22–23, 77–78, 87, 93–95, 117–32
Marxism and the Philosophy of Language
   (Vološinov), x, xv, xxi, xxii
Masturbation complex, 53, 54
Materialism, xviii, xx–xxi, xxiii. *See also*
   Dialectical materialism
Matijašević, R., xvii
Medvedev, P. N., xxi, xvi–xix, xxiv n.8
Messer, A., 68
Metaphor, 104, 116
   gesticulatory, 104
   intonational, 103–104
Monadology, 124

Monism
    materialistic, xviii, xxii, 119–20, 123, 124
    spiritualistic, 120
Myths, 57–58

Nekrasov, N., 113
Nietzsche, F., xxii, 8, 31, 32, 68, 76, 137, 138
Nihilism, 127

Obscenity, 58
Oedipus complex, 41–44, 47–48, 54, 57–58, 59, 61, 80 82, 90 91, 136, 137, 139
    as an ideological formation, 82
Optimism, 76
Overdetermination, 141–42

Parmelee, M., 18
Pavlov, I., xx–xxii, 18, 83, 129, 130
Peer group, 137
Pfister, O., 72
"Philosophy of Life," 12
Physiology, 21, 22, 34, 71, 83
Piaget, J., x
Plato, 89, 138
Pleasure principle, 36, 40, 42, 44, 52, 121, 129, 130
Poetics
    sociological, 97, 109
    theoretical, 93 94, 95, 116
Pragmatism, 12, 13
Prague Linguistic Circle, xv
Preconscious, 29, 37, 48, 70, 72, 134
Projection, 140, 141
Psyche, 120, 122, 127, 131, 134, 139–40. *See also* Conflict of psychical forces; Conscious; Dynamics of the psyche; Preconscious; Unconscious
    content of, 24, 82–83, 86–87
Psychoanalysis, xiii, xix–xx, xxii, 7–10, 17, 22–23, 25, 30–32, 72–73, 133–135, 136–39, 140–41, 142
    ideological motif of, 9, 10, 17, 50, 68
    and Marxism, 117–22, 123, 125, 127, 129–30, 132
    theory of character types of, 71–72
    theory of culture of, 7, 17
Psychoanalytic treatment/therapy, 43, 54–55, 64
    as a social interrelationship, 78–79
Psychological aesthetics, 96–97
"Psychologization of the somatic," 71–72
Psychology, vii–ix, x, xii, xix–xxi, xxii
    objective, viii, ix, xxii–xxiii, ۱۹. 20,

22–23, 67, 70, 78, 86, 118–19, 123, 125, 140
    subjective, 12, 18, 19, 20, 25, 67, 69, 73, 75, 80, 83, 118–19, 120, 123, 124, 125–26, 127

Rank, O., 8, 31, 32, 41, 43, 59, 62–64, 72, 82, 120, 139, 140, 141
Reactology, 18, 118–19, 120
Reality principle, 36, 42, 44, 72, 130
Reflexology, xx–xxi, 18, 23, 128–31
Religion, 7, 58, 77–78
Repression, 35, 36–37, 39, 44, 46, 55, 137, 142
Resistance, 50–51, 54–55, 80

Sakulin, P., 93–94
Satire, 112
Saussure, F. de, 135
Scheler, M., 12, 13–14
Schelling, F., 124
Schopenhauer, A., 30, 31, 32, 45, 68, 73
Scientific creativity, 87
Semiotics, x, xi
Sexual, the/sexuality, 10, 14, 35, 82, 90–91, 120, 121, 129, 137–38
    and age, 10–11
Sexual instinct, 10, 39–45, 46, 121, 129, 133. *See also* Eros
Sexuality, infantile, infantile, eroticism, 40–41, 51, 71, 81, 82
Simmel, G., 12, 13
Slip of the tongue, 55
Smirnov, S. D., vii
Social environment, ix–x, xi–xii, 86, 133, 135, 136, 138–39
Social forms, 60–61
Social/ideological values/evaluation, 96, 97, 100–102, 107, 108, 110, 114–15
Sociology/sociological method, 21, 22, 24, 93–94, 95–96, 97, 109, 116
Socrates, 138
Spengler, O., xxii, 8, 12, 14, 137, 138
Stern, W., 68, 124
Strachey, A., 139
Strachey, J., 139
Structuralism, xv, 133, 135–36, 138, 140, 142
Stumpf, K., 68
Style, literary, 108, 110–14
Superego, 46–48, 59, 60–61, 76, 78, 136
Symbols, dream, 51–52, 142
Symbols, erotic/sexual, 59, 90

Tetens, J.-X., xxii, 68
Todorov, Tzvetan, xviii

Tolstoj, L., 59
Tragedy, juridical theory of, 113
Transference, 43, 122, 134, 137, 140−41
Trauma of birth, 62−64, 82, 139, 140
Tropisms, xx−xxi, 83
Trotsky, L., 117

Unconscious, ix, xi, xx, xxv n.18, 24,
    29−30, 31, 32, 34−37, 39−41, 43−44,
    45−48, 49, 51−54, 62, 69, 70, 72, 77,
    80, 82, 118−20, 121, 125, 127, 130,
    131, 133−35, 140

Verbal discourse, xxi, 79, 83, 93, 94, 96,
    98, 105, 109
  in art, 106−107, 116
  and extraverbal situation, 98−101, 105
  participants of, 103, 104, 105, 109−16
Verbal reactions, 21, 22−23, 26, 34−35,
    79, 85−86, 87−88, 127

Verbal utterance, x, xii, xxi, 76−79, 86, 88,
    127, 140
  behavioral, pragmatic, 98−101, 103,
    105−106
  in literature, 106−108, 110−12, 115
Vološinov (Voloshinov), V. N., viii−xiii,
    xv−xxiii, 133−35, 136, 137−42
  attribution of works to Baxtin, xvi−xix
Vygotsky, L. S., ix, x−xi

Watson, J., 18
Weininger, O., 13
Wish fulfillment, 36, 51
Wundt, W., 18

Yaguello, M., xvii

Zalkind, A. B., 118, 128−32
Zinchenko, V. P., vii